HOME IS THE ROAD

HOME
IS THE
ROAD

WANDERING THE LAND,
SHAPING THE SPIRIT

DIANE GLANCY

 Broadleaf Books

Minneapolis

HOME IS THE ROAD
Wandering the Land, Shaping the Spirit

Cover image: moopsi/shutterstock
Cover design: Olga Grlic

Print ISBN: 978-1-5064-7477-9
eBook ISBN: 978-1-5064-7478-6

CONTENTS

Part VII A Moving Point of Reference

Part VIII Nothing but Sky and Ground

The world is a book and those who do not travel read only one page.

—Augustine of Hippo

O public road.

—Walt Whitman

The thorn bush is the old obstacle of the road. It must catch fire if you want to go further.

—Franz Kafka

PART I

THIS VILLAGE
CALLED A RIVER

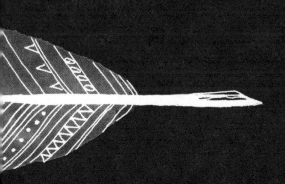

THIS VILLAGE
CALLED A RIVER

A Wayfarer

My life began in travel—a wayfarer not on foot, but in a car.

First trip to the farm was written underneath one photograph taken where I was three months old. We went often. I'm not sure why. I have outlived those who held the memories and there is no one left to ask.

A long time ago I was born in the plainness of the earth. Dust clouds had passed. Topsoil had blown away. The Depression was over. Another war would begin. I was born long ago in the middle of the country in a harsh time. God spoke in the heavy weather. There were labor union disputes and roughness.

We traveled back to my mother's parents' farm sixty-nine miles south of Kansas City on Highway 69. A seriousness was there. My grandparents were remote. I was in the way. They were people to be feared. Now the old farmhouse in Kansas is gone.

The barn and outbuildings. Only the bending weeds in the field still wave goodbye.

I was plain as the words I heard and spoke. I had been marked plain on the assembly line of those slantways where the spirits of infants are dropped into their bodies before birth.

Reading a Mary Ruefle poem, "Sawdust,"—I was trying to take / a nail out of the wall / and it wouldn't stop coming / so I screamed / how much more of you can there be? Jesus then enters the poem as he plays with nails. Christianity came into my life that way—from the beginning it was a story that didn't stop, a story with nails.

In Bible school we learned there were a thousand hills where cattle lived that God owned. My father worked in the stockyards. I thought of God as the yard master. Jesus was his son the way my brother was the son of my father.

Whenever I saw the cattle chutes in the stockyards where my father worked, I thought of church and steeple where we were told we were separated from God. Jesus was the long and dusty farm road back to God. Everyone at Bible school accepted Christ as their Savior. We were scoured. Wiped of anything interesting. Thumbprints. Footprints. Pawprints.

> In those days, we always were moving. My
> father was transferred from plant to plant.

I am starting late on the roads into my own
life. Haunted by a herd of nightmares.
My salvation has been this: travel.
Travel and the Lord Jesus Christ punctured
on the cross.
I am strengthened by the history of my driving.
I would leave the past behind, but it catches
in my trailer hitch.
The former rain has fallen. The latter rain is
still dripping from the eaves.

Gathering Water

On the wall above my writing table is an Edward Curtis
print of an Apache woman filling a round clay vessel
at the riverbank. Behind her, two ponies, a brown
one and a white. They are wearing blankets over their
backs, and basket panniers, in which the water vessel
would ride back to the encampment.

On the table is the actual clay artifact—an early
form of the canteen, flattened on one side to ride
against the hip. It looks like a small head. There are
two handles on the sides like ears, and a spout that
looks like a mouth saying, oh.

One evening, the vessel began to speak. About
how early water carriers could have come from the
full moon in the sky. It asked, Did not the moon come
from the ocean?—Did not a comet once hit the earth
and send a piece of it into the air—gorging out a place
for the ocean to reside?

The Origin of Horse

A long time ago people began to arrive on earth. They wandered from a great distance.

When the people first came to earth, they lived near a river. They built a lodge because the nights were cold. They built a fire.

The Maker made buffalo for the people to eat. But the buffalo would not stay in one place. The people argued with them, but the buffalo would not listen. They called the buffalo a name that is hard to translate, but meant something like, balloon on its back.

When the people traveled away from the river to hunt buffalo, they cried for water.

But how to carry the water from the river.

Many people died of thirst until a woman had a dream of how to form mud into a ball—a round, hollow ball with an opening like a mouth. She dipped the ball into the river and carried away some water.

At first the water ball was hard to carry and slipped from the woman's hands. She made handles on its sides so she could carry it. What is the name of that?—the people asked. The woman said—A-ball-full-of-water-so-we-can-follow-the-buffalo. The women helped her make more balls to carry water.

But how to carry the water balls when they were full of water. It took many people, and the buffalo were far ahead. The people tried to drag the water balls on the ground, but the water spilled. They tried to roll the water balls, but the handles caught in the ground and the water balls broke.

One night, the woman who made the water jug had another dream. In the dream, she saw an animal who said its name was horse. She told the others what it looked like. Four legs and a head something like the buffalo, but smaller. They took clay along the riverbank for a brown horse, and the clay they found among some rocks that was almost white. In a sacred ceremony they breathed into clay nostrils and the horses snorted. They always are snorting to get rid of the breath so they can return to the river clay from which they came.

The women wove blankets from sheep's wool dyed with rabbit bush and the trader's vermillion for the backs of the horses, and baskets for panniers to hold the water balls for the people as they traveled.

They painted the horses in a sacred manner. They named them, carriers-of-the-burdens-given-us-in-a-dream. They called them, carriers-of-water-in-vessels-from-this-village-called-a-river.

The Spigot of the Quarter Moon

What shall I equal to thee, that I may comfort thee.

—Lamentations 2:13

I can't comfort you directly [the past is gone] but I can comfort something in the neighborhood of you and that should help comfort you.

I've always had a depression of sorts—a disturbance I've had all my life. It's more like a disruption of *settledness*—a general feeling of being made of parts that didn't fit with one another. I was born moving between two cultures, neither of which went together, yet my parents stayed married all their lives. It was an in-between place between disruptions I orbited as a child. During my own marriage I continued the orbit, and in the more than thirty years of singleness after that marriage.

At my writing table, I thought of the moon after it was torn from earth. Its jaggedness must have been shaped by travel—by the friction of rotation. Is it not the same with my writing that begins with tearing? Is it not the same with my travel? Aren't those book projects and poems a moon that keeps the earth from tilting too far one way or the other in its orbit? Isn't the moon scarred by craters from the comets that hit it?

Yet it holds its own in the sky.

Does not the moon change the shape of its stories? Isn't it only visible where the light of the sun hits it? The earth often is in the way. Maybe the moon is angry. What does it know of itself?—a satellite in the sky. No more than a clay vessel with a mouth. But thirst and a need for water is our source of life.

I think of the shapes that do not fit, and orbits and movement, and in them is the shape of my own being. Yet I keep trying to make a unit of these indecisive pieces.

The Origin of Water

I have used similitudes.

—Hosea 12:10

In the church I went to as a child, I heard stories. About how Jesus came as a fisherman—sometimes awkward as a clay vessel full of water. The two handles on each side too small for my fingers.

I heard this story, but not in the words they said. I heard Christ was a wayfarer and transgressor who came to tear up the world. The gospel was full of water. It kept us afloat. Jesus walked on it sometimes under the moon. In his travels, he made the gospel. My ears were shaped like handles when I heard.

Farm and road and steer and moving and Bible school stories. There have always been swift disruptions. A clan of disparities. A moving herd of buffalo. A fragile hope less fragile each year. Within the disruption is another. I am torn between my will and the Christ. I follow both. I camp beside one then another on this long journey.

Sometimes I see how far away I can go to see if I get back.

Don't you remember when you could see what you were thinking?—It was a horse song, which is a similitude of truth buried in a story. It was the last trip to the farm. It was a cemetery on the Kansas border where we went to spread the ashes. The land stark as gravel.

PART II
ACTS OF DISOBEDIENCE

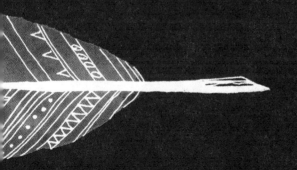

ACTS OF DISOBEDIENCE

The stars are the tracks of Raven in his snowshoes cross-
ing the sky.
—Smithsonian Institute, Arctic Center Studies Exhibit,
Anchorage Museum, Alaska

If I was to go anywhere, it would be with what I could think.

Traveling in my car, westward, not leaving it, day and night, except for gasoline and something to eat. To hold the world together in the car is to drive from northeast Kansas to wherever I'm going. To live in Kansas is to be equal distance from the coasts. I can go east or west with the same fervor and spend the same time getting there.

The rest stops become familiar, pulling in after dark for anonymity and invisibility so it isn't obvious I travel alone. The larger rest areas have room for long rows of cars, which there are every night. The new motel without rooms. It must be the economy. Buffalo herds seeking water, further on. Stopping to rest.

Often, there are railroad tracks nearby.

This is a country of travel—of trains running everywhere along major highways. There are places that say, no sleeping. Other places limit cars to a four-hour stay. I look for the blue signs—Rest Area 2 Miles. Heat is the only thing that keeps me from sleeping in the car, though it cools down once I stop late at night. Once in snow, the snow plow plowed around my car, leaving it buried in a mound of snow. That rest stop was west of St. Louis.

Once, a flock of geese flew above the road. I saw their white undersides, their black wings beating a narrow corridor against the sky. In that moment I saw the visage of a pattern. I imagined the universe as a Mobius strip. In my boltings, I could move on and on without stopping. On a Mobius band there is no end of the road.

Traveling by myself for a long distance makes a vacuum that draws the voices of the land into it. I drive until there is a vortex, and I am in a different realm. A long journey is a small, black hole in which the land, the past, the possibilities of imagination are stuck.

It would be too much to catch the mind moving the way it moves on its errant path. A little ship on a stormy sea. But I am camped at a rest stop, locked in my car after driving all day. I can't sleep but listen to the rain on the roof of my car, the trains that pass, and the trucks that pull into the rest stop, or leave after a few hours' sleep. They grunt like a herd of restless animals. It is my thoughts that can't sleep, but rise and fall from the sea, which thinking is, an endless pattern of memories, associations, driftings, and tempests.

I travel alone. That's where the voices of the past are. I drive—trying to reach something going farther away—and if I reach it, it's not as it was, but changing even as I hold it in my hand. It's like the sound of a plane overhead going somewhere. It is still there, in the air, just farther away, out of reach, changing until it reaches its landing.

This is what I understand from the land and from rocks I pick up during travel. I am not able to see the earth as it is except in brief moments because of the grief it would cause. I would hold that early feeling to my face if I could. I would enter again those brief glimpses of return. It seems sometimes the older I get, the farther away I can see—both back and forward.

If I am quiet and traveling by myself, and have asked to hear what is there to hear, the road offers voices—and thoughts of what should be written.

This is what I know. I was created. I suffered loss. I was restored. I keep traveling both back and forward.

I have a memory of Bible school as a child—there was a lost sheep on the flannel board. There was a feeling it was me, and Jesus left the others to find that lost sheep that was darker than the others. I thought, or maybe it was the lesson, that Jesus wanted his sheep with him. Later, I read the gospel and found a verse in John 17:24—Father, I ask that these also, whom you have given me, be with me where I am, to see my glory which you have given me because you loved me before the foundation of the world.

In that mix, or mux, or flux of language, where phrases run together, and meaning is buried, is the explanation of what I feel. Something other calls me to itself.

Diligence in my work—whether teaching or writing or driving. Certainly, there is the work ethic of my mother's German/English heritage—the way things should be done—which I didn't always receive happily from her.

Once, she pushed me out of the house. I must have been six or seven. I don't remember what I was doing to get in trouble. I sat on the front steps in the dark, except for the streetlight on the corner. I remember the man next door walking down the street. I sat against the post of the front porch to hide my punishment.

It was my father's undocumented and marginal Cherokee heritage—a distillation of what he was, and could not be in the world he lived in to earn a living, to migrate into the world he found to migrate into, and had to move forward in, according to its ideas of punctuality and getting with the plan and achieving goals.

He was circumspect. He provided for us. A steady influence. Always there, until his death. And some-times when I travel, I'm aware of him and more than him. He had a recognition of the being that is the land. He was in church with us. He may have been the reason we went. I also remember his respect for me. It has informed my life. Somehow it came through in the discordant house. Now present in the car, on the road, in the weather and the land.

ACTS OF DISOBEDIENCE

*And when they called in the apostles, they had them
flogged. Then they were ordered not to speak the name of
Jesus, and let them go. As they left the council, the disciples rejoiced that they were considered worthy to suffer
dishonor for the sake of the name.*   —Acts 5:40–41

In dreams, in passing off to the side—in peripheral
vision—I often find what I know. Even though I
have lost the ability to see in the shadows, yet I can
recognize it as similitude. Often it waits at rest stops
when I pull in for the night—the neighbor would
never see me there—sitting on the porch-step in the
dark. That is my definition of Christianity—a hiding
from trouble.

I have aloneness. Though at times I feel the
traveling-beings, the helpers, who like to travel around
me and with me, confident of their presence. Recently,
someone asked if I minded driving after dark on my
long trips. I said without hesitation that helpers are
there on the road at night. There's an endurance or
resilience in the spirit world—when endurance is
necessary. There's a presence that comes, even if it
is only an attitude from within.

I am not a scholar to explain it. I am not a full-
blood anything, but a mixed-blood in a car, heading
away and heading to and trying to find the lost puzzle
parts in an intricate pattern that appears to me in the
creative field and sometimes just in the fields that I
drive past and through. The voices bond together with

all the other voices—is usually what I find. It is my past that the voices find. It is my past and their past where the voices connect. It is where I have found place for the mulling over inconsistencies, contradictions, injustices, the silenced, the effort to reclaim, to tell, to be heard, to connect with the fabric of imagination, which is where stories and the act of writing reside.

My creative scholarship is on the road by myself, sometimes within the shadow of other cars. When I am working on a project, I am following the trail of some historical character. The land has memory. It keeps a journal of what has passed upon it. It is in the elements—if I stand there long enough. There is something in the solitary that I find its shape and connection to the past.

Maybe our memory is found in the land. I remember because the land remembers.

This stone will be a witness to us, for it has heard the words of the Lord he spoke to us. —Joshua 24:27

This is what I know. This is something the land itself has said:

They shall dwell safely in the wilderness, and sleep in the woods. —Ezekiel 34:25

When I am alone at rest stops—when I am alone in the wilderness—the language of the Bible is a trail I follow. How can I explain this to those who inhabit the colleges and universities? In those places I am the odd woman out. The one who stops in the woods. The one who sleeps in the wilderness. It is written. That's how I know I can do it—reading about those old desert travelers in the ancient words.

Words are existence. Language is a living being, especially the voice in motion when storytelling. Our existence and language are inseparable. In the beginning of Genesis, God spoke the world into being. The old ways of oral storytelling—the orality of making as it happened—has changed. Now the word must be written.

The first writing was the making of marks that conveyed meaning. Mere words that looked like animal prints in the earth, or sticks or scratches or marks on stone or papyrus or scraps of hide. Or elk antlers or deer horns scraped against a tree. I've heard biblical scholars say that Seth, Adam's third son, was the one who began to keep written records.

That old betrayal, the spoken language stuffed into written form. The agony of the voice no longer on its own, but carried by those inferior marks on the page. The disappointment of the voice when it found it had to be carried in written words that needed the mediation of reading. How it diffused the story told, the words that rode on the wings of air directly into the ear.

Yet the written words also have enlarged ways of seeing—the extended forecast—this thing is like that. Without written words, how would I know that an Inuit once saw the myriad of stars, and said they were bird tracks?—Or how could I see bird tracks in the snow, and say, "They are stars?"

I do not live in the Native community. If I did, it would be Tahlequah, Oklahoma. But I am aware of the long Christian history there, where conferences began with "Amazing Grace" sung in Cherokee. My great-grandfather was a fugitive of sorts. He fled Indian Territory after getting into trouble. He set up a momentum in the family that has lasted these three generations. I still want to move, to cover my tracks. Stay low.

The prophet Elijah moved in his chariot of fire—my forerunner. My somewhat community is Christianity. Scripture is my Rand McNally Road Atlas. Writing about it are the stones that hold me down and give me place.

You may not want to hear, but I would say I prevailed. I was sent away on my own without any means with which to make my way. When I was torn. Desolate. I knew a state of momentum. To this day, I can drive seven or eight hundred miles a day and sleep in the wilderness of rest stops along the interstates.

Jesus was pushed out of the house also. Like he did, I can sleep and not be afraid.

He found him in a desert land, and in the waste howling wilderness; he led him about, he instructed him, and kept him as the apple of his eye. —Deuteronomy 32:10

It is the Judeo-Christian heritage I'm talking about. Maligned. Despised. Rejected. No comeliness that would appeal to anyone. *Yet my sword is bathed in heaven—Isaiah 34:5.*

If it is true Jesus alone was given for the salvation of humanity, why isn't it more obvious? Why can't I leave it behind, as others have? At times I thought it couldn't be true. The gospel—the good news of death for life.

I had a colleague who wanted to remove the cross from the campus chapel. Another wanted to change our days to a calendar based on something other than Christ's death on the cross. But here we are still in the year of our Lord.

I could not bolt as yet. A child's options are limited. I had two heritages as big as ocean masses with a causeway between them. Within that narrow road, I drive and keep driving.

The land speaks. The clouds. The wind. The river. Sometimes the fog on mornings above the lake and rivers. And voices that were here. I hear mainly voices that did not have a chance to speak. Voices of the unwanted. When I travel, I hear them—in my drivings over the land, unfolding what is folded there. Their voices tell the stories.

I am defined by land—but I have been cut off from the land. Removed from a particular place.

Removed from place, my sense of place is the journey. I have lived in many places over the years. My identity is in its moving fragments.

It was my father's Cherokee part that was a dangling participle—a modifier that didn't quite fit the modified. When I was a child, the Cherokee lived in Oklahoma—as if they lived there only when I was a child. But, it was as a child I heard this, and it modified what I knew of the Cherokee. When I started writing, it was to pin down this floating part of my identity.

In the few trips we made to my father's mother in Viola, Arkansas, my grandmother sat silent. She never came to our house. She died when I was eleven, before I knew what to ask. But when we visited her those few times, there was a sense of erasure—a sense of distance from something else. Our voices were a necessary distance because something was there that couldn't be looked at. Something my great-grandfather had done made him run. There was an unknown history between us. Something not to be asked. Something unanswered.

What was I within the erasures, between the ocean masses? It was in elementary school in Kansas City, Missouri, where I recognized the outcast status I felt on the front steps when my mother pushed me from the house. Maybe I was looking for something other than what she didn't want.

Look to the rock from which you are hewn—Isaiah 51:1. Sometimes I hear the old voices in the rocks I pick up. I listen to what sticks to me—like seeds on the legs of my trousers and socks when I walk in the woods—beggar's lice—someone said those seeds are called.

This writing is for the hidden. The disappointed. Those who continue to keep moving. Voices of the unwanted that we can hardly hear but are all along the roads I travel.

I was willing to be an eyesore in everything I did. Why?

Christian? Why?

I found myself believing more all the time, even as I heard around me, We'd gotten beyond Christianity, thank goodness. Christianity, with its unwanted threat of hell. And other problems are manifold. The fundamental precepts of Christianity wear thorns.

On the road instead of the pew. Or in the pew, if pews could be seen as east-west interstates—I-90. I-80. I-70. I-40. I-10. I think that's how each pew in church should be marked.

I like these troubled waters—these watery roads where I get in trouble, where things break apart, and I hold onto the broken pieces of the boards. We all are here to break apart, to fall desperately into the cold sea.

Give me a church, and I always placed myself on the back row, ignored. Yet I raised two children, became a professor, and made two independent films, wrote book after book, took road after road, which took more faith and endurance than sitting in a church.

After church on Sundays, I visit with an aunt nearing death. She never went to church. "Jesus is Lord," I tell her, though she does not hear and is unable to answer. It seems a secret message, sinister in its covert action.

Does God pluck those he chooses from the doomed and let the others perish? I have these questions that stretch throughout my interior landscape, a travelogue of inquiries. An album of discontent.

Protestant Christianity. It has been foundational in my life—even its incomprehensible and off-setting parts. I believe in the Christ who was crucified.

One afternoon, as I sat with my dying aunt, I think there was a flurry of activity in the room. I was alone with her, but others were there, though I couldn't see them. She had said as much anyway, when she still could communicate. Her sister always was there, though both her sisters were dead. By the time the dying gets to the mysterious place, they can't talk. They can't tell us what they see as that world becomes more visible.

Come now, and let us reason together.   —Isaiah 1:18

Who among us shall dwell with the flames?   —Isaiah 33:14

Reading Isaiah, I recognized a book of many directions—a record of current events, which is now history—prophecies, visions, warnings, promises, invasions, narratives of battles and of captivity. Isaiah continually goes back and forth among them. He must have written on the run, or at least on the move, as he goes from one subject to the next. In fact, isn't the whole Bible a conglomerate of many voices, times, and places? Aren't there many jumpings here and there?—though they all seem, to me, directed on a certain road.

Sometimes I drive with them.

Later in the winter, I flew to Alaska for a ten-day writing workshop. The Native participants, who were mainly Inuit, came with the desire to put into writing their oral stories and the abuses from missionaries / boarding schools—and the alcohol/drug use that rampage their villages. I like to think about the shape of voice as it moves into the written word, even in suffering. The snow-covered trees and the frost in the air also wove their voices. When the workshop was over, I flew from Anchorage to Seattle to Kansas. In Seattle it snowed on Sunday. I like a plane as it rolls down the cleared runway, scattering snow, even when it's a runway not used to snow. I always imagine the plane on a crank and pulley as it lifts from the earth, as though someone above was pulling it toward them. The setting sun made a small fire through the brush of clouds on top of the horizon. Then the gray wing lifted over clouds and turned slowly away. It is in those times I feel the vast, blank spaces inside me. It is what I cover with the fabric of my words.

KANSAS

According to [the physicist Richard] Feynman, a system has not just one history but every possible history.

—Stephen Hawking, *The Grand Design*

My life has continued in travel across the roads before it.

There is land and sky and the car passing between them making a small rip in the passage as it goes. The moving car unzips the sky from the land. I remember this from my childhood. The oppressive life in my house opened to the land, providing a passage.

In the early days, my father was transferred to packinghouses across the Great Plains. Slaughterhouses, they were called. The cattle entered, [1] cut off from the land. They were killed—[2] the slitting of sky from land.

There were other hollow places between parents. [3] Feudal and [4] futile. The starkness of their lives. The land. The sky. The grass between them.

My moving life continued moving as my father's transfers continued: [5] Kansas City, [6] Indianapolis, [7] St. Louis, [8] Reading, Pennsylvania, [9] Kansas City, [10] St. Joseph, [11] Denver, [12] Chicago, [13] Sioux City.

My great ship of exploration was a moving van. [14] Atlas. [15] Mayflower.

I had more than one beginning. I have travels from multiple beginnings. [16]. [17]. [18]. [19]. [20]. [21]. [22]. [23]. [24]. [25]. [26]. [27]. [28]. [29]. [30].

Kansas is named after an Indian tribe. The name means [31] people of the wind, though I remember hearing it also meant [32] blue smoke from Indian campfires on the prairie.

In travel, I become the moving place that distance is. Driving the land has every possible history encamped in rock and stone and soil, and voices smack against the windshield. Smackie. Smackie.

Have I ever known who I am—except in the placement of thought in travel? Travel is the establishment of a moving place, allowing a space between storms and thunder. I can be [33] one place, then [34] another.

Travel is a map, with pins making connections. A group of correlations in the [t]rip.

My mother was born in Hume, Missouri, on the Missouri/Kansas border. I live in Shawnee Mission, Kansas, on the Missouri border. My father was born in Viola, Arkansas, under the Missouri border, and died in Sioux City, Iowa, on the Nebraska border.

As the car moves, the past is exhumed. It is a travel of associations. [35] Exhaust and [36] exhumation. [37] Pastward and [38] forward to every possible future—

WRITING IS A JOURNEY

Similitude is the backbone of writing.

Writing is a journey in a field of horses. An impractibility. A disobedience. If lightning strikes, the horses run everywhere with possibility.

Writing is a rock outcropping containing stories in its layers.

Writing is a hunger. A harvest table set with bowls of different foods combined in different orders.

Writing has many voices and dialogues within. I read Ronald Takaki's *A Different Mirror: A History of Multicultural America* several years ago—about the many nationalities that make up America. But he didn't mention the mixed-blood—the many voices within the one voice that writing is.

Writing is a cocklebur. A bramble. A briar. You walk in the woods, hoping one will catch on your shoes or your pantleg.

And out of Zebulun they that handle the pen of the writer.
—Judges 5:14

Writing is a journey on the open blank road of Kansas. But as the car moves over the road, it becomes the landscape through which the journey moves.

Passing over the road loosens the structure in place—the old rebellions, the chaos at the root of our being we shape into structure. The simple terror of its existence within us makes us search out structure, even as the road unzips the space between land and sky.

It all travels with me—the structure and the chaos. The land somehow draws it out. What is this blankness of the road? How is it the edges of the fields are scraping the car?

The metaphor for travel is first elk or caribou. Then bird or whale. A disembodiment from earth. Stars always were available at night for destination. There was elsewhere in momentum. The way an airplane or a stamp can travel.

Travel is a place of belonging. And I have a sense of belonging to words that drive down row and row in books. Separation is my inheritance. A wayfarer. A traveler by myself. Even to my very bones, if bones could be seen as an interstate highway system.

I wake groaning from a night of dreaming where the past was running. I heard, "You will not have what you want. You will be the last. You will be unnoticed. Grief will fill you. It will wake your sleep. You will be an outsider. This will be your lot. You will feel it in your shoes." The divided heritage. The being undocumented. Being in two places. Living in a house that would not thaw, but left little cold islands on which I stepped. Stepping from island to island, they slip from my feet. I wake sinking into the cold waters. Groaning is the distress I hear from my mouth. I cover my mouth, but a voice can speak without a mouth. I think they hear it on the other side of the wall.

Once the spring on the garage door flung part of itself against the back wall of the garage, barely missing the car and my head.

The story has an artificial interior. A fictional setting for fiction. A likeness. A similitude of what it is getting to. All that is in the way of the real has to point to the real. That is its job. That is mine.

When you wake with the core of yourself.

There was no ceremony. No stories. All that the sedate Methodist Church required of us was the repetition of the Lord's Prayer, Sunday after Sunday. And the same dismal hymns. The words of which I sometimes misread, and would say an s when there was no s.

When I tried to sing, I mispronounced words, or sang other notes, as I could not read music or have a voice for singing. The hymns went on and on through my childhood and adulthood. What if heaven were a continuation of this?

And still, down the road, there in the distance, came the shepherd looking for lost sheep.

It didn't take long to meet the ceiling. I was out standing on the roof of the house, the roof of the church. History came up through my dreams, and scripture called me to an unseen world. I knew myself to be dust, breathed into by the breath of God.

I was tired of the middle of the road my mother said we were.

I am tired of the church revival tent that leaves its weight, even after it is gone.

I come from dust and the breath of God.

PART III

A CONTINUANCE OF TRAVEL

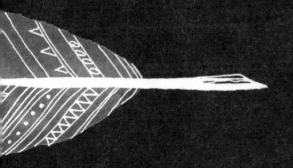

A CONTINUANCE
OF TRAVEL

One morning, during a trip from Kansas to San Diego I saw a bright-red blood spot on the black sky as the sun started to come up. Soon, in the rearview mirror, I saw the top of a mountain was red. "What's the problem?" I asked. Travel brings out a frankness. A coarseness. A meanness. I find as I drive long distances—I am impatient with anything not moving.

In the dark sky the next morning, I saw fringes of white clouds sweep the mountains under them. It was that way leaving a rest stop in eastern Arizona. The stub of a rainbow hanging between the mountain and dark layer of sky.

There are road signs along the desert—Dust storms may exist. It was January 24 along I-10. Tattered ribbons of low, white clouds hung over the road 138 miles east of Tucson. Some of the rolling mounds in the desert looked like whales surfacing. The squat shrubs and small bushes on the desert mounds were the whale's barnacles.

Sometimes, in the distance, I saw blowing sand, as if the southwest was picking up to move away.

Sometimes, the dust swept across the road in strings like the snow I remembered streaming across the highways in Minnesota when I lived there.

Ford Dry Lake Road. Sutro Ditch. Rollie Ditch. Ghost Ditch. Quartz Ditch. Texas Wash. Bula Ditch. Red Cloud Road. Hayfield Road, where there is neither hay nor field. I drove through the desert, past the slow-moving traffic of the mountains. They seemed to roll sometimes like waves on a great, silent sea.

I passed more signs—7,335 feet above sea level—5,000 above—as I passed on my way down to sea level in California. Then Buck Mountain Road. Flat Top Wash. Holy Moses Wash. Rattlesnake Wash. Franconia Wash. Proving Ground Road.

For they shall pasture and lie down, and none shall make them afraid.   *—Zephaniah 3:13*

In 2011, I drove twenty-seven thousand miles, passing several times across the country, east to west, north to south. In January, I drove from Kansas to a conference in southwest Texas, and then to an independent film festival in Duncan, Oklahoma. In January, I drove from Kansas to an independent film festival in Green Bay, Wisconsin, then to western Iowa on my way back to Kansas. It was 4°F the night I slept in my thermal sleeping bag in the back of my car at a rest stop just inside the Minnesota border. I also was covered with my insulated *army-tank* coat that covers head to toe.

In March, I drove from Kansas to St. George, Utah, crossing the Rockies in snow.

In May, I drove to the New England Young Writer's Conference in Middlebury, Vermont, and then to New York City to work with the Mixed Phoenix Native American Theater. In June, Detroit for a poetry conference. In July, Texas, and then Head-Smashed-In Buffalo Jump in Alberta, and finally to the University of Montana in Missoula. August, Tempe, Arizona, for an independent film festival. September, Glen Rose, Texas, and then to Muskogee, Oklahoma, for the Five Civilized Tribes Story Conference. In October, Deadwood for the South Dakota Bookfest, and then to San Diego. In November, Kansas to Florida, and then Los Angeles and back to Kansas.

Travel and research—to ferret voices and images from the land. To write, in other words.

Often, when I return from a long driving trip, I'm overcome with a sense of depression. It takes a few days to recover. I'm overwhelmed by the enormity of crossing the county, maybe in the same way Meriwether Lewis did not recover from his 1804–1806 Corps of Discovery. There's a stalemate after returning home—[it always is the enemy]—the mail to pick up, the groceries to get, the lawn to mow. All those ignored duties become jumbled when they're ignored too long. I'm not sure how not to keep moving.

HOME IS THE ROAD

At times, I feel a slight tremor in the engine of my car. In California one morning, I felt a slight tremor in the earth under my car. The uncertainty we travel on. The uncertainty we trust to be certain.

A DRIVE ACROSS THE COUNTRY

In 2012, in my early seventies, I accepted a new teach‑ing position at Azusa Pacific University, in Califor‑nia. I had been retired from teaching since 2005. After retirement I taught at Kenyon College in Gambier, Ohio. I thought that would be it. But *Keep Moving* is stamped on my feet.

That May, after a conference in Middlebury, Ver‑mont, I drove back to Kansas in two days. I had one day at my house to do laundry, to go through mail, to get things in order and pack again. Then I con‑tinued on the road to California to find a place to live while I taught. It was another trip I made in two days of travel. From Kansas to Tucumcari, New Mex‑ico, from Tucumcari to the outskirts of LA. After I found a duplex in Monrovia, I continued on west to UCLA across the 210, the 134, the 101, the 405, to the Sunset Boulevard exit for a workshop on my fourth play, *The Bird House*, that Native Voices at the Autry produced. As I was maneuvering the curves on the narrow, uneven lanes of Sunset Boulevard, with the directions to the Guest House in my hand, looking for a certain street where I had to make a turn, going farther than I thought I should be going, frayed, disheartened, holding my own, though going slower than others around one of the many bends on the fast-paced road, a young man passed me and called out, "Why don't you learn to drive?"

THE MOVE

Later in the summer, the mover said he'd be there early, but it was 10:00 before he arrived with his nephew, a veteran or a veteran internally burdened with the wounds of duty. They loaded the truck with what I was taking to California from my house in Kansas. They next went to my small cabin on the Lake of the Ozarks in Missouri, which had not sold, but I was emptying it anyway. Then we would drive to Texas to leave some furniture with my son and daughter-in-law. Then to Monrovia, near Los Angeles.

I hardly had left my house in Kansas before he called. The truck was smoking, and he had to return to the shop. I thought of my file boxes. My new printer cartridge, new reams of paper, my clothes, luggage, furniture, books. All my work was in that truck—my writing projects-in-progress with pages of handwritten notes, and the syllabi, which I had just completed.

While they were loading, the nephew informed me he had seizures. "Is it legal to drive with seizures?" I asked, but he said he had a license. I prayed for the nephew before they left—"Heal him, God." Now I prayed again—despite a driver with seizures and a flaming truck with all my work that could not be re-created. Lord of risk. Lord of the crossroads. Lord of ambition, have mercy.

I drove on to the lake. I ate at a Mexican restaurant on the way, where they had pictures of cock fights decoupaged into the table. When I arrived at my cabin, I sorted through the boxes I had packed, and waited until 9:00 that night when the movers finally arrived. Fluid had been leaking onto the brakes and caused the smoke. I went to my brother's house for the night and left them to load the truck.

The next morning, at 8:30, I drove to the cabin. They were still asleep. I knocked on the door. They had fished in the dark after they loaded, catching the large carp that lives under my dock, and then letting it go. I had noticed the fishing poles in their truck.

One of the hottest summers on record. Already we were sweating. Did they want to follow me? We looked at the map. See—the shortcut from Big Cabin, Oklahoma, to Sherman, Texas. They didn't need to take I-44 all the way to Oklahoma City, then south I-35 to Texas. No, they had GPS. They didn't need to follow. I watched the loaded truck climb the steep drive from my cabin. Then I swept the floors, thanked God for the place for the years to write, and locked the door.

It was 109°F when I passed through Eufaula, Oklahoma. The fields were full of dead grass. The trees had turned brown in the drought. The whole earth felt like it could go up any minute. Naked I come into this world. Naked I may leave.

Midafternoon, there were clouds in the sky. But nothing more than a drop or two splattered on the windshield—pungent with the heavy smell of dust. I had the thought—maybe there was a country church nearby praying for rain.

When I arrived in Texas that evening, I called the driver. They were still in Oklahoma. They had missed the turn at Big Cabin. They arrived about 9:00 p.m. After unloading some of the furniture, they were going to drive on. It was a Thursday night. They'd be in California Friday night or Saturday morning at the latest. With the two of them, they could drive straight through. But I couldn't get there until Saturday night. It would take me two days to drive. I had the key. I knew where the furniture went. Could I draw them a floor plan? They asked. Give them the key. I could, and did. We looked at the map again. I showed them how to continue west on highway 82, then 287 through Wichita Falls to Amarillo, where they would connect with I-40 to California. They drove off in the dark.

I took a shower and went to bed at my son and daughter-in-law's house. I could not sleep. There was a full moon. I got on the road, driving with 169,000 miles on my car. God—is there even one moment I do not need your help? I looked for the tail lights of the mover's truck on the dark road ahead, but did not see them.

Around 3:00 a.m., I stopped at a rest area and slept a few hours. At 6:00 the next morning, driving through Memphis, Texas, with four buildings along the highway, I was stopped by Officer Jolly for doing sixty-one through a forty-mile-an-hour zone. The fine would be $183. I had two weeks to mail it in.

The next day, I called the movers and told them I was on my way and would catch up with them. But they were back in Oklahoma. They had to stop in Oklahoma, they said. They had missed the turn, they said. What turn? It was a straight shot through Texas.

The movers still behind me I could spend time in Tucumcari. I exit at the Tucumcari Convention Center, exit 335, as if there would ever be a convention in Tucumcari. Years ago, I attended the Grace and Glory Bible Church and came to a church camp of sorts, a revival.

Killing time. The first stoplight in Tucumcari turns red. Oh good—that will take up two minutes. I drive along old Route 66 that runs through Tucumcari, past decaying motels and closed restaurants. I find the library. Get online. Have lunch at Del's.

After I fill the car with gasoline, there's nothing else to do. I get on I-40 west, and pass four patrol cars, one in the median, one stopped behind a car, two roaming the east and west lanes. I should have warned the movers.

When I call them again, I ask how they are doing. Not good. A highway patrol car had stopped them at Tucumcari to inspect their papers. There is a mandatory ten-hour rest for long-distance drivers. The officer looked at their logbook. There was no sleep rack in the truck. They had to stop. The officer escorted them to a motel in Tucumcari.

In the afternoon, I stop at a large rest area east of Albuquerque. There is shade in one of the far corners—and a breeze—probably from the passing trucks. I close my eyes for a while before I drive across the rest of New Mexico into Arizona.

That night, I sleep at another rest area—just east of Flagstaff. The next morning, I stop at the Starbucks in Flagstaff and spend several hours online again, details for the college. Then I look at the map to find a place to meet. I call the movers again. I wait in Arizona for them, at the exit for Williams. We meet. They will follow me to LA and not get lost again. But they are slow. I get too far ahead of them, and they are gone again.

I wait at another rest area. I call them again. We meet up again in Needles, California. They want to rest. The truck is slow in the heat. One mountain pass was marked, seven thousand feet. They'll get an early start Sunday morning.

I stop at a rest area in the desert of California on I-40 east of Barstow, and laid my head on a pillow a moment. A two-day trip had turned into four. My car was old. It was 105°F. How would they find my duplex on their own with a GPS that took them north when they should go west?

I was lost in the desert. But Christ of the wilderness had gone before me.

I have many Bibles, starting with a childhood Bible given to me at confirmation in the Methodist Church. I have older Bibles that belonged to my grandmother, my mother, my aunt, and an uncle. In 1971, I bought a Bible with a Morocco-leather cover. It is the one I used when I went to the Grace and Glory Bible College, and attended the Grace and Glory Tabernacle. It was what I would call, a thorough church.

The pages of my Bible from those years are lined with notes. They are written in the margins, upside down on the bottom of the page, crosswise across the top. Some of the handwriting has bled and is hard to read. Many of the pages are loose. But the notes stick with me. Beside Psalm 102, I had written, A rejection psalm. Jesus was a heavenly being out of his natural place. Beside verse six—[I am like a pelican of the wilderness; I am like an owl of the desert]—I had written, a root out of dry ground. I felt this way crossing the desert on a move from Kansas to California.

The local movers I decided to use had gotten lost. Their truck had broken down. I felt the root, the dry ground. And the spark that held me. I drove on.

I arrive in Monrovia early evening. I enter the empty duplex with a sleeping bag and pillow I put on the floor. I sleep.

The movers arrive on midmorning on Sunday. They unload. I write them a check. We pray at the table. We say goodbye.

Monday, I get a new phone number.

Tuesday morning, I open my front door at 7:00 to find the mover standing there. He had to take the nephew to the VA hospital in Long Beach for his seizures, which he says the hospital calls, episodes. When the doctor induced a seizure, the scan did not show brain waves coming from the usual place in the brain that seizures come from. Maybe it was the load of memories the nephew carried from Afghanistan.

The mover wants me to take him to a bank where he can cash the check I gave him so he can have some money. We get on the 210 in morning traffic. We arrive at the bank in Pasadena an hour before it opens. We go to breakfast at Russell's, and he tells me of his childhood, and the troubles he's been in, including jail, and how he decided he had to get straightened out.

God, bless the people with lives that are one long drive to California after another.

Oh, God of mercy—have mercy on these men who brought their fishing poles in the truck—the mover and his nephew, whom he tells me only came because he wanted to fish in the ocean.

INTRUSIONS

In academia the world of form and structure is disassembled through language. In my field of poetry, some of the fragments don't seem to fit together. In class we read poems that have unknowable parts, new poetry, nonrepresentational, much like abstract art. To abstract is to place the finding of meaning on the reader.

Now I know in part, but then shall I know as I am known.
—*1 Corinthians 13:12*

The new, elliptical poetry often makes language do something that does not make sense, except for the merest hint or suggestion of meaning. Maybe the world as a whole is too big, and we need to see it in pieces.

How does one read the poetry of inference? How does one approach the inference that poetry is? Sometimes I return to my own file cabinet for directions, which scripture is.

During the semester, I spent time in Ezra and Nehemiah—the books about the return of the remnant of the tribes of Israel after their captivity in

Babylon to rebuild the temple and the walls of Jerusalem in the fifth century BCE.

> *Many of the old men who had seen the first house when the foundation of this smaller house was laid wept with a loud voice; and many [of the young men who had not seen the former, larger foundation] shouted aloud for joy, So that the people could not discern the noise of the shout of joy from the noise of the weeping.*   —Ezra 3:12–13

It's the same mixed message new poetry gives us. The old foundations have been replaced. Not replaced—but sidetracked the way I see long trains across the desert waiting for an oncoming train to pass.

I need the two ways of going. I put Stephanie Burt's *Close Calls with Nonsense* with side panels of Ezra and Nehemiah for a semester's mulling. I need the weaving and unweaving at the same time. The going and coming of traffic on the interstate.

I have seen the inner torments of parents, aunts, uncles, at the end of their lives. I have witnessed their passage. Their crossing is something they could forgo, but it was there for them nonetheless. Before I left for California I visited their graves in two cemeteries along the Kansas/Missouri border. I remember their journeys. That generation is gone, and there are only a few of mine left.

Why did faith seem clear to me, and not to so many of them?

A CONTINUANCE OF TRAVEL

The new poetry questions language and asks questions—how do we know what we know?—and how do we know if we know it? How can we be sure of anything—especially language? New poetry moves the way fragments of dreams move through the head. How different the dream state. How difficult to go without dreaming. Isn't it like the moon that keeps us balanced in our orbit?

During the semester, I had a dream that a train ran through the back edge of my yard. On the train, an open car held prisoners of some sort. Terrifying men without shirts and bald, and they turned to look at me, standing in the yard. Their look was a malicious intent. I knew I would not survive if they were loose. I went in and told my father to tell them to go away.

At the time, I was writing a manuscript of the narratives of the 1875–1978 Fort Marion prisoners about an early beginning/continuance of Native education and evangelization. I was wary of the descendants. The getting into areas I did not belong. Trespassing into other lives, which I have done and done. There would be trouble. I had put the manuscript down again and again, only to pick it up and continue writing. They were men of evil intent in my dream. They had ravishment on their minds. Was the dream of the train warning? Or only my own fears?

Somewhere in the film, *Life of Pi*, there was a scene in a storm; Pi uncovered the tiger so it could see the majesty of God on the sea, but the tiger could not bear the sight, and Pi put the partial cover back on the lifeboat, and the tiger retreated. There is flesh in me that cowers before the living God, broken as you are in my understanding—deconstructed into Jesus and the Holy Ghost—making the trinity even harder to explain than elliptical poetry.

God, I deliver myself to your mercies. I am full of intrusions from places other than you. They visit me daily. I have a will opposed to yours. Sometimes I pray, "My will be done."

When I pass the stinking feedlots in southwestern Kansas and the Texas panhandle, I think of the animal sacrifices at the temple. Lord, I feel your meat hook in my bones.

"You don't have to like it," I tell students as we study contemporary poetry, "but you have to know it's there."

So the wall was finished.   —Nehemiah 6:15

While the remnant of Israel was rebuilding form, my semester readings in new poetry were dismantling form. "Elliptical poets are always hinting, punning [I want to say pruning away words that would be helpful in understanding meaning], or swerving away from a never-quite-unfolded backstory. They're easier to process in parts than in wholes," writes Stephanie Burt in *Close Calls with Nonsense.* "Fragmentation, jumpiness, audacity, grammatical oddities, rebellion, voice, some measure of closure: Ellipticist."

I come to you, God, through fields and roads and sometimes swerving away from a never-quite-unfolded backstory. How I would like to map my way the way I plan trips, charting roads, measuring the shortest way from Kansas to California. Yet for you, I have to travel a road I'm not sure of, yet trust it is going where you are there to meet me, as you have been with me in life. It almost is more than I can do—to walk that road toward you, who have not shared yourself more than saying, I am with you always, even to the end of the world—Matthew 28:20.

Elliptical poetry comes as a synecdoche—a part used for a whole. Or metonymy—the name of one thing for that of another. Not directly face to face. But shadowed. Fogged in like a ship in the bay, one can only see the barest outline of—probably one of the railings [for a synecdoche]. Or I want to say, sailings [for a metonymy]. A substitution, which creativity often is. The railings taken from ships as pickup sticks. Taken by faith, of course, that the rest of the ship is there.

What makes me think I can use the words of Ezra and Nehemiah? I am not of their race or nation. Yet I have community with these oddities.

All scripture is given for edification. —2 Timothy 3:16

Though you were cast out to the uttermost part of heaven, yet will I gather them from there. —Nehemiah 1:9

I too am broken, bifurcated, a stranger in a strange land. Yet I approach you, God, post-Babel, in a muddle of separate parts and on various roads. I am inhabited with a strange exuberance where it doesn't make sense that exuberance should be.

THE TRIP TO KANSAS

It is 1,555 miles from the duplex in Monrovia, California, to my house on the eastern border of Kansas. It's uphill all the way—at least, as far as Flagstaff. Then I-40 descends into the Great Plains.

At the beginning of the trip, not fifty miles east of the duplex, California rises from nearly sea level to 4,257 feet at Cajon Summit along I-15. I see the highway head up the mountain. The trucks growling like herds of slow, lumbering animals.

At Barstow, where I-40 departs from I-15, there's a road sign—Wilmington, North Carolina, 2,554 miles. I'm not going that far.

Traffic on I-40 turns like the electric windmills over the high desert, the trucks and cars moving east and west, except several out of step, turning a little slower than the others—their blades up when everyone else's is down. Now there is snow on the mountain tops. The altitude at Flagstaff is 7,335 feet. Now down into the flat slab of the southwest through eastern Arizona and New Mexico with a rise and fall into the bowl of Albuquerque.

On the second day at Tucumcari, I cut northward on single-lane Highway 54—across the upper corner of New Mexico—across the panhandle of Texas and Oklahoma into Kansas. Somewhere on a back road, I heard a radio preacher talk about angels and pronounce the word, *cherry-bims*. All day, I drive behind cattle trucks and a line of long-distance carriers through scattered small towns with forty-mile-an-hour speed limits. It's four hundred miles from Liberal, Kansas, on the southwest edge of the state, to my house in Shawnee Mission, Kansas, on the northeast edge of the state.

I pass a train carrying new windmills, disassembled. The long, humped blades are a pod of whales along the railroad track. I pass a line of oil cars like black hogs on wheels.

Lord, I am plain as alfalfa. Subtle as hay and straw. My magic wand flickers and goes out. My wild horses have run away. My cow. The chickens followed.

I want to say Hallelujah to lift my exuberance. I love the drive from California back to Kansas. But the first day at least—from Los Angeles to Tucumcari on the interstate—before the second day turns to endurance. My words begin to burn. Someone touched them with a match—It's those cherry-bims all wired up.

Excuse me, Lord, for following you so closely. I've read the driver's manual—a car length for every ten miles an hour the vehicles are moving.

A CONTINUANCE OF TRAVEL

Lord of the brush clumps, make the road swift and greased with your grace. I need your radiance. Oh God, my holy effort. Of whom the world was not worthy. And I come jumping to you with my trip unmended.

THE TRIP BACK TO CALIFORNIA

When I have purpose on a long journey, I can't sleep for long. I have lain awake too many times in motel rooms just waiting to get on the road. Often now, I pull off in a rest area for a few hours. When I drive two days from California to the eastern edge of Kansas, and two days back again to California, I stop in one of the rest areas west of Tucumcari for the night—part of the night. I lie down in the back of my small SUV, knowing my vulnerability.

On the road, I cover the passenger side of the front seat with a blanket as though someone was sleeping there. I cover the driver's side before I lie down in back. I pin strips of an old sheet to cover the back windows. There's a GPS aerial on the back of my car, though it's not been activated. No one else would know.

For darkness comes into the head and into the dreams of the head on the bed, as Daniel said in Daniel 7:1. It is enough in itself that no robbers should come with it.

Thanksgiving break and driving from California to Kansas. On Thanksgiving Day I drove to Texas, where my son lives with his family, and arrived after dark. I drive because I don't belong to the families of the children. I feel an outsider. Not one who belongs. A solitary traveler so I don't have to visit awkwardly with the group. I want the road alone. I will be who I will be. I drive the land back and forth.

I think of the pilgrims. Their journey to the shores that could have eaten them, and many of them did not survive. California to Kansas to Texas to California. The stark history of the country. The brutal wars with the Natives as the country took the land to form a significant nation.

On Thanksgiving night the stars forget to fly.

THE BIRD HOUSE

They fracked the land until all we got left is the size of a bird house.

—Rope, *The Bird House*

I

Native theater is an old story. The acts of the incoming on the structure in place—that is, the Native Americans as they were when the European culture came and disrupted their way of life. The slaughter of buffalo, certainly. But just as definitive was the disruption in the form of storytelling that was root to Native survival.

Those who came into the country were explorers and frontiersmen, first of all, then the cavalry. Then the settlers who established their ownership on the land. Then the missionaries and zealots with their story of calvary. How close those two words, calvary and cavalry. How alike their meanings. Overrun. Stamp with a structure of another until we are not-our-own and not-one-of-them either. Destabilization. Removal of one's structure and the imposition or replacement of another mysterious and painful to it. Why shouldn't that show up in the displacement, frustration, and anger of Native plays?

Christianity has been central to the Native American. It is the main religion, though divided among denominations that hardly seem related. Many Natives are against Christianity, as it was a supplanter of language and culture. The boarding schools were mainly punitive. I wanted to look at the painful.

Fundamental Christianity. Holy Ghosters. The born-agains. A belief that Christ took the sins of the world upon himself and carried them to the grave. Those who believe are free of sin that would keep them from heaven. The different faiths divided the different tribes. Catholics. Lutherans. Baptists. Presbyterians. Moravians. Methodists.

What a strange place, America, with its commercialism and altruism. Its capitalism and religious fervor. Its extremes of weather. Its conglomeration of different cultures.

The clinging of some to Christianity—to the gospel message that Christ bore the sins of the world on the cross. It doesn't make sense, but it is a life force.

A rehashing of my life in my own voice overset with a critical look at Native theory, I wrote the play, *The Bird House*, produced in the spring of 2013 at Native Voices at the Autry, the Autry National Center in Los Angeles. The play contains what I think of Native American dramatic theory and methodology, and the process of writing a play. *The Bird House* is written from a minister's troubled perspective. Give your characters all the trouble they can handle is the mantra of playwriting. Then give them a little more than they can handle. What arises thereafter is their character.

In *The Bird House*, I wanted to capture the largeness of the past and of the land in a very small place. I wanted to catch Native history—not preaching about what happened to it, but showing it in terms different than what is expected. The way contemporary art is often indirect—peripheral.

II

As I travel, it is windy in the Great Plains. It feels, at times, as if a large hand pushed the car. On my trip from California to Kansas, I pass through Greensburg, Kansas, that was leveled by an EF5 tornado in 2007. The town largely has been rebuilt. Greensburg, Kansas, population 1,574 in 2000. It was only 777 in the 2012 census. It covers 1.479 square miles. A small town like Ropesville, Texas, the setting of *The Bird House*. Both Greensburg and Ropesville, diminishing with each census, are something like Native tribes wiped out by disease against which they had no immunity, and if that wasn't enough, they then suffered the takeover of the incoming civilization.

III

In *The Bird House*, a man discovers his mission when expectation is turned upside down.

The situation: Reverend Hawk [whose name is actually Jonathan Logan] is pastor of a small church in Ropesville, Texas. The downturn in the economy sends his congregation to Lubbock and larger, surrounding towns in search of work, while the need for energy sends drilling towers and the method of fracking closer and closer to the church.

The complication: Reverend Hawk's sister, Clovis, and half-sister, Majel, live in the backroom of the church. When the board sells the parsonage to pay bills, Hawk removes some pews and moves into the balcony of the church.

The crisis: What do you do when you believe in God, and God is silent? What do you do when your life feels like the size of a birdhouse?

The epiphany: The land is fracked by a method of drilling that endangers groundwater by forcing carcinogens into the ground to break up shale beds that cover the natural gas. Reverend Hawk is fracked by the loss of his church. Clovis is fracked by a stroke. Majel's Native heritage is fracked by assimilation. Even Christ the Savior, Overseer of all from the Christian perspective, suffered fracking on the cross.

The exploration of an environmental issue: At one point, Rope explains the fracking process to Reverend Hawk: "You've seen the arrival of those drilling operations, Hawk. They come as if they're going to mow the pasture, but they shave the grass down to the dirt. They dig a large pit for water. They drag in their trailers. They put up a wall around the site to hide what they are doing. Then the drilling rigs arrive. You hear the growl and screech from the tower. You feel the earth wretch. They jab it with their poison spear—over and over. Hydraulic fracturing. It fractures a path into the earth. They'll get the same back." Rope is a local cowpoke of sorts, a watcher of happenings in Ropesville. He is one of the few men who attend Hawk's church.

I remember watching the convoy of trucks when I visited my son, who lives in Texas. I stood in the field, listening to the noise. I heard the bawl of cows in the pasture. Even they knew something unnatural was happening.

My son's house is supplied by well water, which now contains bentonite from drilling. They cannot drink the water, but make trips to Walmart in Decatur for the plastic, gallon water jugs, which now crowd landfills in state after fracked state.

IV

The play began during a conversation on a patio under hanging birdhouses. At the time, I had three old relatives. I remember asking if I could write a play about aging, stroke, loss, diminishment—all the grimness. Of course I could. *The Bird House* would add land pollution from pesticides and drilling for natural gas in West Texas. Once I began writing, I hardly stopped.

After a word enters the page, the words keep growing, much like the mud that grew on the surface of the water in an old Cherokee creation story. As the first draft takes shape, I saw this particular play was about three characters struggling for their economic survival—Reverend Hawk; his sister, Clovis; and their half-sister, Majel, who is half-Native.

There's more to the Cherokee creation story. At one time, the animals lived on a sky rock, but it grew crowded, and they fell off the rock to the water below, and drowned. One animal finally swam to the bottom of the water and picked up a piece of mud and placed it on the surface of the water, where it began to grow.

But it stayed a clump of mud until a bird—usually the vulture—flew over the mud to dry it. Where its wings touched the mud, there was a valley. Where its wings lifted, there was a mountain. The land became the "turtle island" of our continent because, in one version, the mud was placed on a turtle's back that was swimming in the water there.

The "fall to the water below" is where a play begins. The characters are in a difficult situation full of tension and conflict, which somehow will be resolved with character change and epiphany.

By the third or fourth draft, the author, him/herself, is the vulture beating his/her wings over the mud clump on the pages of his/her play. An author has to be willing to drown, because there at the bottom of the water, is where the "stuff" of the play is.

The church board is thinking of selling the parsonage, then the church. The sisters, Clovis and Majel, live in the backroom of the church. It is a constricted place where their lives grow more constricted. Of course, since this is Native theater, the church represents the reservation and placement of the characters into the loss of a way of life. Hawk also struggles with his understanding of Christianity and God's purpose in his narrowing life.

Full of birds. I almost could hear them in the background of the play. Often, as I wrote, I could hear a morning dove on the roof, and other birds in the backyard. Somehow, I was led to reread *Black Elk Speaks* by John G. Neihardt, about a Lakota holy man at the end of the nineteenth century, who faced the end of the Plains Indians' way of life. I saw my own little play as a re-version of facing "the end." And I could ask in *The Bird House*, what possibilities are waiting there?

Black Elk Speaks is a book full of birds, from the geese that first appear like arrows in the sky to speak to Black Elk, which led him to an understanding of the Plains Indians' "end times," which was a real "end time," not just a forecast—to other birds, such as the spotted eagle, grouse, crow, magpie, chicken hawk. Reverend Hawk is an afterimage of Black Elk, who was left with an enormous sense of failure as he faced his holy visions. From grimness to grimness. What more could I do?

In Texas, I've heard the drilling. It is a violent rape of the land. How else is there to say it? A pipe driven into the ground, breaking the underground layers to get to the natural gas underneath.

Restoration doesn't come, but more loss. Throughout *The Bird House*, Reverend Hawk "does battle" with God [as the rapper, Eminem as B-Rabbit in the movie, *8 Mile*, "does battle" with his words at rap competitions].

After his trials and his difficulties that do not end with the end of the play, Jonathan Logan is a dignified man caught in an undignified time as Black Elk. He achieves the nickname, Reverend Hawk, which he always has been called, as Natives [usually historically] have changed their names according to some new accomplishment or change in their lives.

For an undercurrent of the story, I took the Native-American-on-the-reservation experience and placed it in a church in Ropesville, Texas, surrounded by the overuse of pesticides and fracking. A Native play that doesn't look Native. I wanted to break down the walls of what is expected in Native theater. On a reservation, life often grows smaller through poverty, alcohol, drugs, the lack of hope and opportunity. In this play, the church suffers the loss of its congregation, the sale of the parsonage, and finally the church itself. It's a new rendition of the Native experience of downsizing. It's Native theater trying to explain the upheaval its culture has faced.

Dislodged. The congregation is dislodged by the economy. The church is dislodged by its loss of members. The land dislodged from its natural state. Native theater is dislodged from its usual place. America is dislodged from its moorings. We are dislodged from part of ourselves.

V

Nadine Gordimer and J. M. Coetzee are two white South African writers, who write very differently about apartheid. Gordimer writes directly—It's wrong for foreign people to come into a county, establish their society, and marginalize the Native peoples. Coetzee says the same thing, but wraps it in fiction. In *The Heart of the Country*, he writes of a daughter and father on a plantation of sorts, when the father, a widower, returns with a new wife. The daughter is closed out of their lives and clumps around the house, trying to get back into her father's life, with disastrous results.

"This play isn't Native," was one of the first comments I heard after a staged reading. But it is.

I've written more traditional Native plays. This time, the Native play doesn't look Native. What is expected in Native theater? How many times do I have to explain it to others as well as to myself?

VI

Downsizing, cutbacks, change, and loss of a lifestyle. That is Native history, after all—a way of life reduced to a reservation.

Will everything keep diminishing until we're living in a birdhouse?

With a conversation on a back patio with the birdhouses hanging from the eaves, we spoke of questions around aging, stroke. One of my three old relatives was still alive as I reached the end of the play, nearly three years after I began. She always said something out of left field that gave me the idea of Clovis speaking after her stroke—that interesting interior landscape. I wanted a sense of language that oral tradition is— words are the main characters. It is words that are the actors in the orality of Native storytelling.

So much of the play came from my trips to Texas—ideas for the dialogue came from walking in the country where my son lives. Each time I drove to Texas from Kansas, I had more. My daughter lives in Kansas. It is where I will return when I finish my stint in California. I pick up large parts of the play on the edge of his Texas pasture. Images. Thoughts. Impressions. Stories.

Bless Jared, Clovis's son. Help him with his children. Help him to market his bird houses. Show him your patterns. Title them—Laid Off. Hard Up. Job's Loss. Uzville.

Bless the drifters that come by the church. You tell us to leave a few stalks in the field for the wayfarers. There seems to be more of them all the time.

I've made trips to rural Texas to visit my son and daughter-in-law in their troubled marriage. I've made trips after they made their peace together. My fourth grandchild is in Texas, where cows yowl at sounds of the drilling for natural gas. Where pollution from pesticides harms the land and its creatures further.

VII

A Native play is an alignment. It's a story of its own story. But *The Bird House* was the story of the land I heard as I stood on the edge of the pasture—a girl pushed off a swing. Hawk telling his own memory as the board assessed his church.

Maybe it was the land telling me, the author, it was being pushed out of where it belonged. Maybe it's the story of us all.

A play is an alignment. An alignment—yet a dislodgment. An alignment of dislodgment and disruption. How can such awkwardness and oppositions be?

Native theater is about the breaking of a culture that was its own world—and what comes after?—other than the fragmentation in which I speak.

Native theater is an attempt to put itself back together in a world in which it does not belong. A world alien to its being. While Europe spent its centuries developing the outward of culture: refinement, education, civilization, the Native American—the Indian—developed a stream of story-telling—stories that could last for days—stories that connected the tribes to the ultimate being of the universe.

An alignment of discordances. A dislodged alignment. How can the breakages be addressed?

Native story storytelling is a breaking into a larger world. Old Native storytelling was a migration. A journey to understand the world. Though it was a limited world—a small world—it aligned its language to the universe. An alignment of the smaller to the larger, the way the bottom ends of teepee lodge-poles made a circle on the ground inside the teepee, crossed at the top of the teepee—the smoke hole—and opened to the sky—making an X form when the teepee lodgepoles were in place during encampment.

VIII

In a section of the book *American Gypsy*, I wrote, "Realized improbabilities [is the term that] probably describes the network of possibilities for the unlikely elements of the topography of the native stage."

In *The Bird House*, Clovis suffers a stroke and dies. She delivers a monologue as she passes above the Texas landscape into the hereafter. I like the impossibilities that can be achieved in Native theater. The unlikely realities. The realized improbabilities. Native theater intermingles this world and the other world. It can do whatever it wants in an act of possibility. The land can speak. The sky also.

IX

After I visit my three grandchildren in Kansas—watch their soccer games—pick them up from school—play the game of "Clue," talk to them about their lives, I start back to California. My 2007 Chevrolet turns 194,000 miles on the two-day return trip.

The large trucks on the highway are herds of migrating animals. I love to travel the interstate once I get through the narrow roads of Kansas, the corners of Oklahoma and Texas, and the fifty miles south across the upper corner of New Mexico to I-40 at Tucumcari. Then it's westward on the interstate across New Mexico, Arizona, and the southern California desert.

At one point, the sky is dark with clouds in the distance, yet the mown hayfields I pass are a bright yellow-white in the sun.

At night, the moon is large. Because I'm older and sleep less, I can drive long after dark. I can think about my work. I can listen to the sometimes eerie voices that arrive in my imagination. Maybe they are part of dreams: I am up against them now. The ones who don't think I am here. The ones who don't consider who I am. The ones who came against us. Who sent us into exile from our language and culture. Who put a structure not-our-own over us and changed the vital act of storytelling. The ones who came with the US Army. They came with the missionaries, evangelists. The Christianization of the Native American until what we have is a birdhouse. An artificial structure where birds have never lived before.

Sometimes I take notes as I drive. They are a parataxis—afterimages of the places I have passed— sometimes they take on different meaning when placed in the story I am writing, the way storytelling tells again in different situations.

Sometimes the meaning of a story changes when told again in a new circumstance. Like the denominations of Christianity that divided—or attempted to—the Indian tribes into a likeness of themselves, leaving scars affecting generations.

The longer I drive, the more scattered thoughts become, especially toward the end of the trip, when I feel I am drowning in my heritage of migration across the land.

X

At the Autry production, a Native actor played Reverend Hawk, who is not Native, as, in the past, white actors have played Natives. I liked the reverse appropriation. A Native actor played Majel, of course, and Rope, an old cowboy who courts Majel, was played by a Native—a Native playing a Native. I like that also.

For the set, we used birdhouses in the shape of a church and birdhouses in the shape of birdhouses. It is Jared, Clovis's son, who makes birdhouses to sell. It is his birdhouses Clovis brings with her when she moves into the backroom of the church.

What is a birdhouse but a constriction? But it also is safety from storms and predators too large to fit in the small opening of a birdhouse.

What could be more alien to the Native culture than a birdhouse? What could be more against natural order? Yet what could be more to the point?

XI

For methodology, you travel. The land carries stories it will share if you ask. You research whatever can be researched, and then you listen for the voices—the torn bits of dialogue. They will be hitchhiking somewhere. Or they will show up in the morning after sleep in a car at a rest area.

These roads—these little islands we bring into existence in the great swirling sea.

PART IV

A BOOK OF ROADS

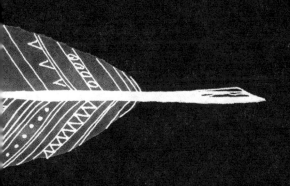

A BOOK OF ROADS

Now it is summer. I make a trip back to Kansas.

In the distance, a train passes, its railcars no more than the size of coffins.

At first there were a few clouds crossing the desert. The few drops of rain had a sharp metallic smell— well water, iron rust, dust.

My car thermometer registered 119°F at Needles on the California border. A few hours later, it was 72°F in the mountains at Flagstaff. Temperature is relative, changing with altitude and time of day. The season. The clouds. All of it has a say.

Along I-40 in southeastern California, as well as Arizona and New Mexico, there are places of black volcanic rock, as though burnt by the sun. By evening, I was in Albuquerque. I kept driving east across New Mexico to a rest stop thirty miles west of Tucumcari, where I slept a few hours. Before dawn, I was driving again. On Highway 54 at Tucumcari, I took a turn and continued across a corner of New Mexico, Texas, and the Oklahoma panhandle. In Liberal, I started on the four hundred miles northeast through Kansas.

After a few days with my family, I drove from Kansas City to Northern Texas, a seven-and-a-half-hour trip to stay with Ray, age five, another grandchild, while his parents were at a conference for their school district.

It was vacation Bible school time in Gainesville. Each morning I took Ray to the First Baptist Church. One day at noon, when I picked him up, he gave me a collage he made, the glue still dripping from the popsicle stick that served as a mast. It was the ship the apostle Paul was on when it sank, as told in Acts 27. I always have loved the story of the shipwreck. And survival after the shipwreck. Paul held onto boards and broken pieces of the ship as it came apart on the rocks in a storm. He reached shore, where he was bitten by a venomous snake, which he also survived.

The ship in Acts 27 is glued on green construction paper. The two white sails are isosceles triangles. One of them, Ray colored with streaks of purple, gray, blue, and red listing somewhat to the west. The other sail colored blue, green, yellow, and orange is more chaotic with sweeps of vertical streaks of color, as if gusts of wind or torrents of rain. Below the sails, and above the roily waves, are a collection of pieces of brown construction paper cut into small squares and pasted to the construction paper in the shape of the hull of the ship. They resemble, somewhat, the armor of an armadillo.

At the end of the week, early on Saturday morning, I left for California from Gainesville and drove fifteen hours to the rest stop east of Flagstaff, near Crater Road. I had stopped at the crater site several years ago, which is fenced, owned by the park department, and allowed access to only by a video presentation in the building, followed by outside observation at the crater from a fenced area, and a guided tour. I was amazed at the control and ownership of a large hole in the ground made by an ancient crater.

It was so hot in the car at the rest area near Flagstaff, I could not sleep, but lay in the back of the car in the sweat chamber. Finally, I must have slept several hours until I woke. The sky was black at 1:30 a.m.

The lights in a small, distant town floated in the darkness.

Half of the moon was in the sky.

The ship my grandson made in Vacation Bible School rode with me in a file box in the passenger side of the front seat as I made the long trip though the heat in the ocean of the night, and the mountains off to the side, which were the rocks along the shore.

I was within the outcropping of trucks, the bedrock of the road along rest areas and parking areas where the drivers sleep for the night, or part of the night. Or some take a stop within their travels through the night.

Atlas Van Lines. Allied. Mayflower. United. Covenant Transport. Fleet. Western Flyer. Pacific States. ABF. Yellow. National Carriers. CRST. John Christner. CTI. C. R. England. IWX. Swift. Titan. Roadway. Freymiller. FFE Transport. DLT Trucking. Conway. Prime, Inc. Transport America. Colonial Freight. FedEx. US Mail.

I also pass large fire-equipment trucks from the wildfires that burn in Arizona and New Mexico each summer. And burn in new fierceness in California. A result of drought. No campfires is a sign posted by the road.

Besides the outcropping of bedrock on the passes, I think the trucks are the ghost herds of buffalo. I like to be near trucks. They also are the animal herds of the road.

It is 59°F at 2:00 a.m. near Flagstaff in the mountains. 94°F at 5:00 a.m. in the California desert on June 30. It will be 110°F by afternoon.

In the dawn, I see a train double-stacked with fifty-six cars. I count them to stay awake. Other trains with four or five engines have too many cars to count.

There is rain falling in the distance or smoke rising.

Now the shadow of the car runs ahead on I-40. The pale sand and sage brush look ghostly in the first light.

My car with 189,000 miles keeps going. When it wants to slow on an incline, I get in the truck lane and let it slow.

In driving is the shredding of the self. I am weary and stretched beyond what I think I can endure. Long travel brings me to this. I drive until I am broken. I cry from the sorrow of driving, from the burdens of a long life. Of endurance. Of knowing I am nothing.

I learn that faith takes me so far. Then it disappears and I am desperate in my hopelessness. In the shelving as I drive, I come to the other half of the moon in darkness. My failure in marriage. As a mother. Maybe

I have been a better grandmother. I am ancient, I think. Where will I go after this? Will there be driving there?

In the heat of the desert, in the ruffle of oblivion, I am on a road that doesn't always stay the same, but its constancy is in the moving.

Jesus—I think—regretted he didn't live in the time of interstates. I think he and his disciples would have been a long-distance truck-driving herd of buffalo.

In travel sometimes distance is relative, as well as temperature. Travel does not seem as long if I'm thinking about something interesting—isosceles triangles, for instance, or how writing is like geometry—measuring shapes on the road, and the relationship of traffic to the variables of passing land.

How long is a mile? Where did it come from? A mile is a long way when driving several thousand of them. A mile is a mile in the prevalence of driving.

From Wikipedia:

A unit of distance called a mile was first used by the Romans and originally denoted a distance of 1,000 [double] steps ["mille passuum" in Latin], which amounted, at approximately 29 inches [0.74 m] per [single] step, to 1,618 yards [1,480 m], or 5,000 Roman feet, per mile.

I pass a cross in the meridian. To me, Christianity means holding onto what has been discarded.

I listen to books and a CD of the New Testament as I travel. Not the diffused Christianity, but the driving-the-hogs-over-the-cliff, arise-take-your-mat-and-walk Christianity. The get-in-your-car-and-drive Christianity.

In June, 2013, I drove 4,170 miles from Monrovia, California, to Kansas City, to Gainesville, Texas, back and forth to Bible school, and finally back to Monrovia for a second year at Azusa Pacific University, as sweat ran like Elmer's glue from the mast of the ship.

In the despondency that comes from long travel through the darkness of the night, I've discovered solid as a ship with two sails is also its cargo of wounds.

NOTES TO THE JOINT STAFF OF CHIEFS

You know all the travel that has befallen us.

—Numbers 20:14

Please do not leave. Oh, please, when I talk about driving and driving the roads. When I talk about why it's time to, and how I see faith against all possibilities. Why it is cogent to me though not others. I have not seen miracles. I have not had visions. But I've held a steady pace.

It began through impossible roads that had not been there. My prayer to God from the beginning— You are the blight I suffer under. You make the world different to those who see it from your different perspective.

My childhood was in Kansas City in the late forties. A man across the street left his family. I knew then that men did not always stay. Though my father did.

We drove our 1949 Ford, faded green, even when it was new, to California to visit an aunt who had fled Kansas. My father took the backseat out of the Ford where my brother and I sat below window level all that way. I suppose my father meant it as a play area, though with no air conditioning in the desert, and nothing to look at other than the back of the front seats, it was a trial of endurance.

My brother and I were cowboy and Indian. All around us, families were in trouble. A paralyzed man repeatedly asked my friend Linda to sit on his lap. A boy suffered rheumatic fever and did not go to school. I passed him as he sat on his front porch. My father went to work. My mother stayed home. I had dreams of being abandoned in a pen of some sort. A platform that held hay for the cows. They could chew my legs when tired of hay.

Mrs. Kenny, the neighbor, lent her hand to our raising. I remember knocking on her door for a cracker as a small child. Their house was the next one on the hill. It sat over us like a large bird. There was a closet in my brother's and my room. I remember it as bigger than the room. How like a closet, the containment of a car when I am on the road. There was sparseness in the house. The way houses used to sit on the ground without bushes or shrubs surrounding them. Yet in my dreams, I remember other floors. Another house on top of the house. I still have that dream.

Methodist church attendance was fundamental and recurring as Sundays to our lives. I liked to hear about the miracles Jesus did. Fishermen became disciples of the living God. There was an outside-the-normal in the Christian faith. Jesus came with possibilities other than current events and whatever they droned on about.

Once I dreamed my brother and I were trees. Leaves came out of our mouths when we spoke. It was strangely horrific in the ordinariness in which we spent our lives.

My mother was raised on a farm. Eventually there was a telephone on the wall with a party line. She had to stand on her toes and yell into the receiver. It is something she did all her life. I picked up on it. I never have been comfortable talking on the phone. It is an effort to make oneself heard.

My childhood was full of chuckholes. They were a cast into which I was poured. Molded. Misfitted. Misshaped. Different parts of wholes.

I would not be one of her. I was one of her. Both were true.

Distances are roads. They are journeys away from one place to another [as in from house to school and back to house]. There is redundancy in the journeys that distances are. A plurality of distances. I work on multiple projects for many years. I wake one morning to one. Another morning to another. They are journeys of distances to place. The cities found there are a restoration of voices. Cities, as in books. As in voices speaking something of what distance is between them. A room of disarray. Of multiple happenings. I will clean it tomorrow.

There is something about driving with traffic moving across the highways while imagining all the other highways everywhere. The separate cars and trucks and transport trucks and recreational vehicles moving of their own accord, though sometimes with a map. They are a structure of the unseen world. A movement of different speeds and opposing directions. A travel of variants on the highway—a microcosm also intrinsic in the macrocosm. The way particles and atoms and molecules move and interact. A march of elements fundamental to the structure of life on the universal level with the movement of planets and stars and solar systems—with the travel of variants on the highways in a miniscule universe. The way the universe is part of the quirks and jerks along the p-brane that cut in front of you. The roads you travel might be the mark of flutons or futons or fundamental differences that speed in a concert of movement. The way cars shuffle onto the highway like particles or molecules from patterns beyond what is there.

The way I sat in the old closet in the room my brother and I shared when we were children, longing for another place. A house we had come from, or were possibly going to. The strip of light under the closet door—a far horizon where I wanted to travel.

THE MARCHING IN THE TOPS OF THE MULBERRY TREES

The most important times in my faith are when I come to nothing.

That's true in teaching also. I set the perimeters of the class—start into the materials, then give them the wheel in small-group discussions, and the final presentations they give. I like to be with twelve students sitting around a long, rectangular table. Talking with them as they ungnarl the meaning of an abstract poem.

I recently came to nothing again. If I wanted to walk with the upright, I had to have a laminectomy—the relief of a pinched nerve in my lower spine.

I often have wondered how people in the Bible walked with, talked with God. More, how God talked to them. Was it an audible voice? Was it a thought?

And the Lord God said to the woman.   —*Genesis 3:13*

The Lord said to Cain.   —Genesis 4:9

The Lord said to Noah.   —Genesis 7:1

Now the Lord said to Abram, Get thee out of thy country, and from thy kindred, and from thy father's house, unto a land I will show thee.   —Genesis 12:1–2

Certainly I have moved place to place. Did I hear, "Get thee to Oklahoma? To Iowa? To Minnesota? To Kansas? To Ohio? To California? To Texas?"

And the Lord said to Moses—

And the Lord said to Samuel, to Nathan and Gad, the prophets—

The Lord said to Jeremiah, to Isaiah, Ezekiel, Daniel, Hosea—all of them.

The Lord spoke to the people in the New Testament too—

The Bible is full of the Lord speaking direction [2 Samuel 5:22–25]—

When the Philistines heard that David was king over Israel, they came to seek him. David inquired of the Lord—Shall I go against the Philistines? And will you deliver them into my hand? And the Lord said to David,

Go. And David smote the Philistines, and said, The Lord
has broken in upon my enemies.

Again, the Philistines spread themselves in the valley
of Rephaim [2 Samuel 5:22–25].

David inquired again of God; and God said to him, Wait
until you hear a sound of marching in the tops of the mul-
berry trees. David did as God said, and smote the Philis-
tines from Gibeon to Gazer.

I want to hear the voice of the Lord speaking of the
sound of marching in the tops of the mulberry trees.

The King James Version actually says, the sound
of going in the mulberry trees.

Van Gogh's *Mulberry Tree*, 1889, looks like the
burning bush on a rocky hill with its orange leaves
against a blue sky. The trunk and ground and sky are
straight brush strokes. The leaves are curling spirals—
possibly clumps of paint furrowed by the small handle
of his brush.

Why do I sometimes feel alone on a rocky hillside,
like Van Gogh's *Mulberry Tree*? Perhaps it is because
it is where I learn both ends of the brush can be
used.

This is the way—walk ye in it—I have heard it over
and over in difficult situations. The verse right before
it says, though the Lord give you the bread of adver-
sity, and water of affliction—Isaiah 30:20.

It is what there is to do on a sleepless night—go back over scripture. Lord of Glory, your ways are past finding out.

I am saddling up for another semester. I haven't finished my summer projects.

One of the projects, a small narrative poem draft after draft, is trying to reach the simplicity it calls for. Wolf Lays Down—it's a street in Lodge Grass, Montana, near the Little Bighorn National Historical Site. The name is from Isaiah 11:6—the wolf shall dwell with the lamb.

We went far in the country to an old cabin
for ceremony.
It always was evening when we left.
The men worked.
We had to wait until they were ready.
At first it was quiet in the car.
To speak would bring the world with us,
and we were going to a different place
from the one we left.
The miles went by.
We heard the low rumble of Uncle Carl's voice.
He spoke the deer and small animals
out of the way—
telling them to wait in the woods
until we passed.
Then he prayed to The Maker.
He made three sharp yips.

Nothing held us to this world
but the rush of wind around the car
and the bumps as we turned onto smaller
and smaller roads.
We arrived at the cabin far in the country.
We were silent a long time
until Uncle Carl let out another yip.
The elders spoke of our long history.
A little group of porcupines guarded the way.
We unrolled the winter count of our people—
alcoholism, abuse, family dysfunction, grief.
We offered our sorrows until the universe curved
like a bow of light in the clouds.
We prayed until the universe was small as the rim
of a cup onto which we slid our pain
and wrongdoing.
We prayed until our sorrows lay down with the lamb.

In science, patterns of the greatest are in the smallest.

I once audited a physics course—in quantum physics, there are variables—particles that become waves, but when they are measured, become particles again. Maybe that's why David should not have numbered the men in Israel—because he put a limit on possibility.

I want to say that teaching is a journey of healing, though I'm not sure. Sometimes teaching is a journey of undoing.

Each day coming, I will have class preparation, discussions that go their own way, writing assignments on which to make comments. I have things to do. Things to figure out. Stories that maybe say other than what they are saying. Similitudes and likenesses—they are my place of belonging. Give me the sound of going in the mulberry trees.

A CARAVAN
OF DAYS

[The ability] to do things without understanding.
　　　　　—*Antifragile:* Things that Gain from Disorder,
　　　　　　　　　　　　　　　Nassim Nicholas Taleb

I used to think moving was an adventure of a new place, and it was. I've moved many times over the years. We always were packing our house when my father was transferred to another packing house location. I remember the empty rooms I left. I remember my new room when the movers opened the boxes. It was like receiving my possessions all over again.

Moving was an opportunity to sort through, discard, start over. Now, as I prepare to move from California, I think the upheaval and change of place must be something different, like dying. Labeling boxes for Kansas or Texas, organizing them in rooms for the movers, reminded me of clearing out my mother's apartment after her death.

There is a lot to do when moving—notifying utilities—Edison Electric, water, gas. Insurance companies. Turning in boxes for cable and internet service. Leaving a forwarding address at the post office.

Notifying magazines, journals, and others places of the address change.

The movers arrive Monday morning. They spend the morning and early afternoon loading the truck.

a queen bed

a single bed and wardrobe my brother made

a chest of drawers

a linen chest that had been my aunt's

boxes of towels, pillows, and comforters

three tables: one for writing, one for course work and grading papers, one for eating

the chairs that go with the tables

a living room couch

a chair that also had been my aunt's that I had reupholstered

pictures, most of them by my grandchildren I had framed

many boxes of books

three small chairs and a child's table I used for a coffee table for the couch where I put my feet when watching television, grading papers, and reading for classes

two side tables

lamps

two small televisions

six small, plastic open-top storage boxes for my work and work-in-progress, which I asked the movers not to stack because they were plastic and would break, but which they stacked anyway, and broke more boxes of memorabilia including a small Navajo rug, three Indian baskets my great aunt bought in Arizona before I was born [in which she watered her violets that leaked into the baskets and placed them in the north window of her place in Kansas, which faded them as much direct light], several old license plates, the hard drive my grandson and I removed from an old computer [otherwise it would have been in Bangkok, my son-in-law told me], the round clay water vessel a friend gave me [like the one in the nineteenth-century Edward Curtis photograph on the wall above my writing desk], programs from many independent film festivals, and three large birdhouses used as props in *The Bird House* at the Autry National Center

several boxes of my collection of rocks

large suitcases with my clothing and several large boxes of shoeboxes

many boxes of dishes, flatware, pots, pans, microwave, kitchen utensils, and equipment

a small fridge the size of an upright coffin or of the water trough on my grandfather's farm

washer and dryer

mop and broom

Late in the afternoon, I start east from Monrovia on the 210 for the two-day trip to Texas. "The weather is cool, and traffic is moving," I say to the movers as we leave. But on I-15, fifty miles east of Los Angeles, I see a long line of trucks stopped on the incline to Cajon

Pass. We spend three hours in traffic as cars and trucks from both directions are rerouted. A bridge under construction is burning, I hear on the radio. Somehow the wood scaffolding caught fire, and the bridge collapsed.

For miles, I see black smoke above the California desert, picked up in a strong wind that stretches it across the sky. As I pass the exit ramp and onto the entrance ramp motioned by firefighters, I see the bow of girders that fell from the mooring on each side of the interstate.

I sleep that night at the Crater Rest Stop on I-40 east of Flagstaff. The next morning, my car won't start. I call AAA. They report I am outside the battery service area. They list my towing options: I could be towed thirty miles back to Flagstaff, or seventeen miles ahead to Winslow. What does outside battery service mean? I wait on the line while the local office talks to the regional. It means they won't bring me a battery. Which tow service do I want? Winslow, I answer. They give me the name of the tow truck owner. I call him. Why can't you just bring a battery? AAA has beén slow in paying. He doesn't do that anymore. Did I want to be towed to Winslow or not? Yes. As soon as he takes he daughter to school, he will be on his way. It was three hours since I discovered my battery was dead to the time he is pulling my car up the ramp onto the tow truck. In the large, rearview mirror of the truck, I watch my car ride along behind me like a horse with its nose to the wind. In Winslow, my car receives a new battery and I receive a bill for $225. There is another $52 bill for towing. I am, after all, only a basic member.

On I-40 road again, I keep driving toward Texas. I stay a night in a motel in Santa Rosa, New Mexico. I see couples all around me in the café. Am I the only lone traveler on the road?

In the morning, I continue on. The workers are still at my place in Texas when I arrive. Their painting cloths on the floor, their tools scattered around the rooms. Ladders and paint cans. The movers are an hour behind me, I tell them. They've had since January. They finish painting. Clean up. The movers arrive late in the day, three hours behind me. They unload and start north to Kansas. I tell them I will stay in Texas for the night. I sort through a few boxes. I sleep.

The next day I drive to Kansas. I receive a call on the road. The movers want to unload. How soon can I be there? It's a seven-and-a-half-hour trip, I remind them. When I arrive, my street and my yard are torn up while a new drainage system is installed.

My house in Kansas also has been torn up. I hired a man to remove the wallpaper while I was in California—three layers he tells me. Then he painted the bare walls. Everything taken down from the walls is still down. Now the movers are moving more furniture into my small bungalow.

My mail, which was supposed to be delivered to my house in Kansas beginning May 1, is not in the box. I have not received a renewal notice for my car tags, which should have come a month ago. I have to visit Social Security to establish Medicare again, and supplemental insurance, now that I am no longer covered by insurance at the college.

I have two places in absolute disarray with 482 miles between them. What I need in Texas will be in Kansas, and what I need in Kansas will be in Texas.

My worry about the hereafter, is that, like AAA, my automobile club, I also am a basic member of the Christian community. I have not been a missionary, or given up my desires in a penitent journey into the desert. I have not fasted often, mostly not at all. I follow my own desires.

On top of all the moving, I have to prepare for a writer's conference in Tucson at the end of the following week. And another conference at the end of June in Salt Lake City. I have to decide what materials I'm taking to each, and line them up in piles with the boxes to be unpacked.

I used to need things in place because I was torn inwardly. I think those tears are still there. But not nearly as large now. I have learned to deal with disruption. I have learned to deal with the broken places.

Life is a process. A long journey. I am a caravan of days just passing through.

Moving is like death, I decide. It is upsetting. It is being overcome with the unknown. A pack up and arrival in a different place. A major move is a little like a journey to a place you've heard is there, but don't for sure until you arrive.

A BOOK OF ROADS

I return to Texas. There's a place on I-35 south of Wichita in Kansas where I get sleepy. I seem to slow down like a child learning to read, but fight sleep and stay on the road.

I pass the hay rolls in fields shiny and slick in the bright sun.

My son lives on a county road east of Gainesville, Texas. He has a pasture for his horses and a barn. Many years ago, there was a pecan orchard on the property. A few trees are left, but most are gone. Half the barn was a store where they sold pecans. There are three large rooms, with torn-up rugs.

When I was in Texas over Christmas break, I hired a construction company to make a bedroom, a study, and an open kitchen / living area in the barn. There is a Pullman-style bathroom with the washer and dryer I brought from California. I have a walk-in closet and built-in shelves. The place had to be rewired. Electrical outlets updated. A new septic system. Furnace/air and water heater. The whole place was in need of redemption.

I hear my grandson playing at the table. We had been to Walmart to buy a toy. His two action figures are struggling. That is the root. We must know it at birth.

In Texas, at night when the moon is full or nearly full—so bright I can see the white horse standing in the open field like a night light.

There is nothing ahead I can see. Nothing I can be. I have no trappings. I am solitary and dazzled on the road against what is bigger than me. My past is like clothes that don't fit. My future is having something to give up for someone else.

These are the mysteries at the end of life. The coils in the tunnel out of here. What it will be? How prolonged? Will it be the same experience as living? I remember upheaval. The birth of two children, my husband changing jobs three times. Sometimes not by choice. The uncertainty. The frustration. I wanted a career also. It would be a long time before I went to the Iowa M.F.A. program, then to a small college that had had all-male faculty and needed a woman and a minority.

Afterward, my life began to open with trips, foreign travel on my own.

Many years ago, during a sabbatical, I spent a semester in Australia. I purchased a dot painting at the Arunta Gallery in Alice Springs—*Snake Dreaming* by Marilyn Armstrong Nambitjinba, Aranda Tribe.

The explanation tale is written on the back.

Long ago, in the Dreamtime, two snake Ancestors fell from the sky. They wandered across the desert searching for a site to make a nest. During their search they made six nests in the ground, but after a time they found them unsuitable and abandoned them to continue their search. When the first rains came, the holes filled with water, and ever since then the waterholes have been providing Aboriginal people in the area with a permanent water supply.

There are three waterholes in the Mount Leibig area, and three at Kintore. The background pattern of dots represents the sand dunes and stony ridges in these areas. The dots on the aboriginal dot painting resemble the small clumps of spinifex grass I saw from the height of Ayers Rock.

When the snakes in the dot painting started bothering me, I went to Walmart for a small jar of art paint. I colored over the eyes. The snake was now asleep. The sting removed.

Why had I chosen it? I liked this one because of its simplicity. The order of the lines. But still it was snakes on the wall.

I can interpret Dreamtime when snakes fell from the sky in that old expulsion from heaven. How art thou fallen from heaven, O Lucifer, son of the morning! How art thou cut down to the ground—Isaiah 14:12. Sometimes scripture swirls around me like a dust storm.

Dreamtime is change.

A move from California. A time to force order on disorder. A time to unpack. I discover a broken leg on my aunt's linen chest. My small collection of license plates is missing. BLZ from Minnesota. WIZ from Kansas. And an old, red Missouri license plate that had been my uncle's. Gone. Gone. But everything is on a migration trail.

PART V

AT DAWN, WHEN YOU DRIVE AGAIN

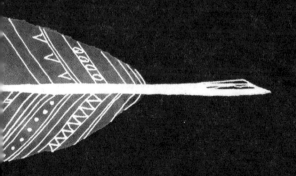

CIVIL WAR SOLDIER AND A GRAPEFRUIT

I am sitting at the breakfast table, eating grapefruit and thinking of my great-grandfather, who probably never had a grapefruit to eat. But he knew grapeshot for the cannons, and the grapevine that told him he could not return to Indian Territory after the war.

You don't usually think of American Indians in the Civil War, but my paternal great-grandfather, Woods Lewis, a Cherokee, was in Company L, Fourth Cavalry, Tennessee, on the side of the Union, because Tennessee was split. He was from Meigs County, Tennessee, where some of the Cherokee lived before the Removal, and there he enlisted.

In the war, he was in trouble, spending time in the brig because he shot a squirrel when the soldiers were supposed to be quiet. Years ago, I found his records in the National Archives. I had spent the morning going over Confederate files, and couldn't find him. I asked for help, saying that my great-grandmother received widow benefits after his death. The clerk informed me that my relative had to have been a Union solider because the families of Confederates did not receive government benefits.

I returned to my table and chair with another microfilm. There was my great-grandfather. It was like talking to him.

After the war, Woods Lewis married a woman from Meigs County, Tennessee. He went to Indian Territory, and after trouble, he and Margaret Blevins Lewis settled in northern Arkansas and had nine children.

Dr. William Jasper Hall helped Woods Lewis apply to the government for disability. On the outline of a man's body, Hall marked places where Lewis suffered rheumatism from sleeping on the damp ground during the war. The medical drawings Hall made also are in the National Archives.

Dr. Hall later married Orvezene Lewis, one of Woods Lewis's daughters. She became my paternal grandmother.

Most of the men in my family have gone to war.

As children, my brother and I played cowboys and Indians. War was with us. It was in our games. It was in our heads.

The Civil War was a war of immense suffering and death—a war of division that lasts to this day, a historical event that defines our country. It also was a war in which thorough record-keeping had a vital part. Scribes followed the troops. Scribes kept daily events that authenticate the details of the soldiers' lives. It was the scribes who unrolled their kits on the ground and wrote with quills and metal-nib pens.

I wonder if Woods Lewis knew a scribe made note of his actions.

Our historical conscience—established in the root, the trunk and branches of our country arose from the tree that was the Civil War. It still seems to fall with the leaves of that same tree. I've heard reports that ghosts have been seen at various Civil War sites. Maybe they are not ghosts, but replays. It may be possible that an archive of everything that has happened in history exists somewhere. A place where records are kept and sometimes slip out and haunt the inner landscape of the fields of war and my imagination—the way you see images on a scrim.

The grapefruit was first recorded in 1750 by Reverend Griffith Hughes. He called it, the forbidden fruit in his book, *The Natural History of Barbados*. By the 1830s, the grapefruit had received its botanical name, citrus paradisi, a fruit of paradise. It finally was called grapefruit because the clusters of fruit on the tree resembled grapes.

I like the opposition of differences—forbidden and paradise—in one small, yellow fruit. The same polarities are in the larger words, Civil War—meaning a war between opposing groups of citizens in the same country—and civil, meaning mannerly, being considerate of each other. The civil act of releasing slavery. The Civil War, with the death of six hundred thousand it took to do it. The great war of 1861–1865 should be called the Uncivil War.

And why did Woods Lewis join the military?—
since the Cherokee were driven from the southeast to
Indian Territory by US soldiers.

What was it like for our great-grandfathers in the
deprivation of war? No wonder Woods Lewis shot a
squirrel for something to eat.

Did the war haunt him as it has other relatives who
have been in later wars? What caught on the scrim of
his thoughts?—a man with his great-granddaughter
looking back at him—without a chair or table when he
ate. Not a grapefruit anywhere.

I drove from Kansas to Washington, DC, to attend
the Civil War program at the Arena Stage.

Before finding my way to the Arena Stage on Sixth
Street and Maine, I visited the National Museum of
the American Indian adjacent to the Capitol. There
I saw an exhibit, *Indelible*, by Larry McNeil, born
1955, Tlingit/Nisga'a. Information posted on the wall
said that his photographs used the historical plati-
num process in contemporary work. McNeil used
this technique to visually scribe that Indians had
not vanished either. His Feather Series was different, close-up and enlarged photographs of sections
of a feather. The rachis or shaft through the barbs
reminded me of a straight road through the rows of
plowed fields in the Midwest. In one photo, the edge
or vane of the feather lifted like the spill of waves.

After the visit to the museum, I went to the afternoon program at Arena Stage, where I listened to monologues about the Civil War, one of which was mine, about his shooting a squirrel, about the grapefruit. After the program, I had a few hours of daylight left, and decided to start back to Kansas.

In three days, I had experienced a reminder of the Civil War. The Indian Wars. Perspective broadened by distance. And drove along the history of the long-fought battle to establish and maintain the interstate highway system in America, much of it under repair as I traveled through Pennsylvania, Ohio, Indiana, Illinois, Missouri.

TOTEM

A Distillation of Peripheral Fields, an Abstraction

Acknowledgment to Gerald Vizenor

James Mackay to Sophia, his four-year-old daughter, when she asks,
"What is the Wild West?"
"Aggressive territorial expansion based on racial bigotry, then justified through religio-cultural imperialism."
—Facebook, June 18, 2015, European University, Cyprus

An opposition within the oppositional. Emote and Mote. Emotional taking to other places by the vehicle of sound in its solid, written form—making large with sound that is spoken when read aloud—that is sounded when an engine runs. But hereafter, *e* removed from emote, making it mote—which is the charge memory has with its many perspectives imbedded in the one memory—making memory motational. Or [e]motational, if you will [in spoken story]. But the *e* after which will be omitted.

Therefore, reclarifying mis-stories mis-told about the Indigenous.

Moting is transmotational—Words in other words. The blocks of language that can be made to turn sideways and go through a space between fences. It's where horses lead. And we find them in another field. A transmotation from the field that is theirs into one that isn't. Or from other memory, from one field that isn't theirs, into one that is.

Likewise, Native migration is traced by the movement of a forward kind. And the Indian is a new being, somewhat squeezed by the passage. A revelation of the American Indian with the up-squeak of motal intent. Not wanting, in other words, the happenings that happened nonetheless. But speaking their stories of who, what, when they are. And how.

Nonetheless is an interesting word. A fact given to refute the previous fact. Another fact has taken precedence. A [trans]precedence, in other words. Transfixed as horses when the oats are connected to them. Their noses in the feed bucket. Because of minimal grass in a winter field.

Who can write about being overtaken by another—without inflicting a bite? There is reciprocity in the offsetting. The nature of nature in an understanding of the crumbled. Oppressed by an oppressor of oppression. A given binomial lifting oppressiveness in a series of oppressionals that negate the slippage from the pasture. But where would they go? The interstates are not conducive to hooves.

It was not a given that erasure would be given. But hidden in the folds of interrelationships of layers between. Loss embedded in language. Of the past we know much. Remembered by the rememberers. Something remains of what was. In the field of horses. In the clouds that pass. In grief that burrows on the edge of the pasture.

The winter trees. A rickety chance at meaning. Branching trees without leaves as they are in winter. But still the grasses flat, fallen down, set up again between the folds of fields after snow in its polarities.

I tell them, stay on the land. Show photos I took of the photos. Making syrup of what is otherwise tree sap. It always is performance of wind on the fields. The pluralities of weather.

It is weathery—would it be right to say?

The full moon a hypertext on the horses in a field. Bustling cattle across the plateau. Pulled back into an outlier. An escarpment away from the wind.

The artifice of what constructs the idea of memory—or the memory of idea. Recounted from different perspectives. The doubling of meaning in the use of trickery to get at truth. The singular of the plural.

Tribal stresses similitude and abstraction. Invent a world of moving herds of language over the continent. Clarified as they are signified in the undertext as well as overtext. The unintentional amalgamation of the disparate. Indian absence and presence, neither coming nor going. It will surprise no one.

There is interiority. Intentionality. A story within a story that transposes the story it is within—and without. A visual understanding of assimilation. An artifice. An artificer making recovering from it.

A totem pole I bought as a child on a trip to California. A force in its own field. A caricature of a tree. It is alone in my memory, but not alone. What storytelling is and how it was taken from the land overtaken by others. The uplifted binoculars to forest, grassland, winding creek. Something remains of what was. Something taken to what will be. In the wilderness of Native thought.

The Native world turns with hurt. Distortion. Wounding. Poverty. Taxation. To which it overplaces transmoting by rightly naming the heretofore unnamed. Or at least mis-named. Overmoting the moting of natural range. Which often happens when angry. Being put all into one box, now calling the boxes, which being opened, spill into one another, each talking with their interchangeable, transmotational parts.

A section of travel that has to be surpassed when another car is oncoming on the narrow road or one-lane bridge of meaning. The swag of road during what have been my travels.

The skewed pieces holding changes of transmotational translingering on the land.

A usurpation in the act of mapping identity.

How does the land remain in a reconceptualized, linear rationale to the still nonlinear post-academic Indian? When not fixed, but transfixed. As I drive, the land speaks of disruption and continuance. The discovered rhetoric of transgenerative indigeneity.

A conflation of causes in the act of carving. Remembering land and what transpressed upon it. Lineage. History. Legend. Of those who came to take, to change, to rename, to carve it as their own. To transmote into the future of what is to come. Filling in history or the parts of it that seem to be missing. Following the resonances in the fields of consciousness—aligning voice to the imaged voices that haunt. A new and settled wilderness. A place to stand.

In the long driving away from the wounding. No, the long travel on long roads brings up the wounding. But it is not the wound. It is the journey through.

IT IS THE STONES THAT SURVIVE

Feelings, acts, and experiences of individual men in their solitude, so far as they apprehend themselves to stand in relation to whatever they may consider divine.
—William James, *The Varieties of Religious Experience*

Go thee therefore into the highways.
—Matthew 22:9

There are wildfires burning in the west as I start another journey. This trip is from Kansas to Banff, for a writing program.

But I don't leave yet, as, at the moment, there is thunder in the distance. This page is my landscape. These paragraphs are my shelters. Until I begin driving.

The lamp, the cord of which has a short, or maybe the outlet, wavers with light. The thunder rattles the house. I feel the table speak—a tumbling of the cargo I thought was held down.

Driving the straight-line interstate the next day, I think of the program I saw on television. *Passage in the Congo*. The red dirt roads were mud, with ruts that swallowed truck wheels up to the axels. Overloaded trucks with cargo packed high. People riding on top. Lopping over roads, trying to bypass trucks stuck in mud. Men digging and digging in the mud that covered the wheels.

At one point, in western Montana, I smell the smoke of distant wildfires. I say a prayer of stones. In wildfires, it is the stones that survive.

In two weeks, with fifteen Indigenous writers writing and talking about writing in the Northern Rockies, at times I dream of driving. The fragments of story interrupt. Imagined events thread with actual ones. The elk graze near the house where we work. Clouds travel like herds across the mountains. Communal voices gather in one's own voice. It is elevation at these heights.

At dawn on the second day of driving after I leave the Banff Centre, south through Montana and Idaho into Nevada, the shadow of my car runs beside me on the embankment along Highway 93. It is a moving petroglyph. When there is no embankment, the shadow of my car drives farther away in the field—a cardstock of sturdiness with a moving image upon it.

Driving is part of my work. In motion alongside the. Vastness I feel the memory of the land. Sometimes as I drive, I feel I am reading. I feel I am being read.

FILMING WHILE DRIVING

The winter coat

It was long ago. You imagine it passing in a car. Memory is that way. You see yourself at the bus stop at the start of fifth grade. You pass as if you are on a long trip, filming the landscape as you pass. You travel alone as you were standing alone, waiting for the bus until it turned the corner, bright as sunflowers along mowed fields you see as you travel. The brown hills fold into one another. The grain bins huddle. The hay rolls graze in a field.

At the bus stop, you wore a new school dress, always cotton plaid with a sash tied in back. It was the beginning of many years before you could buy a small video camera and drive for days until the past returned. It would be years before you knew the places moving in your video camera were your home. Your mother called to you to stand up straight, or don't scuff your shoes. Your father at work. You were part of him. Removed from what you were. Exiled from a place you belonged. It was one of those cassettes you ignored for years.

Later, when you look at it, you see the girl standing at the school bus stop, wearing a coat of ice though winter had not come.

The clouds move like a film across the sky. You stay in the field, thinking of stories. Sometimes a story calls other stories to it. It is what your father said. If you are quiet, your heart doesn't follow.

These fragments that come

This is the sound of the boy's truck as he slows on the road. Rum. Rum. Rum. Waiting to see if you will come to the truck. When you do, he leans over and pushes the door open for you to get in. You have not been in his truck. There is a Pendleton blanket over the seat. The steering wheel is wood. There is a small feather hanging from the rearview mirror.

You see his hands on the wheel as he drives. You see his arms. You see his legs slightly apart. You want to touch his thigh.

He takes you to the bluff on a small hill. You sit with him, looking at the land. His house is the first at the bottom of the hill. Your house is farther away. He does not get out. He does not look at you. He just sits, watching. A hawk flies over. A crow. The sun does not move in the sky. Another bird seems to fly without moving. He starts the truck and drives back down the road. He lets you out at your place.

Your mother saw him from the window.

"What did you do? Where did you go?"

"Nothing. Nowhere." Those are the answers you hear.

She does not say anything else.

There are spaces between the boy's words. You collect the silence. It is part of your own.

You are a witness to the solitude. You say nothing. It sits on your chest of drawers with stones you find in the field behind your house. It sits on the dashboard of his old truck in the dust. It doesn't matter if he doesn't speak. You only want to be with him.

These fragments that come

You are not alone when you wait for the school bus. But you do not speak to anyone. Your brother is with the others. Fussing. Pushing. Shoving. "Hey," you say. This is the sound of your voice when you speak. "Hey. Stop that. Hey."

Hark. Hark. You want to say.

At first, there is nowhere to go but school. The little birds twirp at your window. You close it before you go to the corner for the school bus.

In the meantime, you watch the clouds that hang over your house. You know you are surrounded by them. Beyond the field there are animals there. Deer. Badger. Muskrat. You lay your words on the ground as an offering of pine nuts.

In the morning, you hear rain on the window. It sounds frozen. Peckle. Peckle. That is the sound of the window.

You know there is frost nearby.

These fragments that come is your house. I didn't mean to mess this up.

In the beginning, two small beds against a wall. A chest of drawers you share with your brother. A living room and kitchen in the house. The clothes stiff on the line.

Your thoughts are a little flock of sheep scattering. Where is the sheepdog? Where is its bark?

It would be a long time until you found the road and owned a video camera. It probably would not be in the boy's truck, though you didn't know it then.

[Though you knew it then.]

These fragments that come

At the Indigenous Writing Program in Banff, a woman said when she was in boarding school, the nun smashed her face into a radiator for speaking her Native language, and it broke her front teeth. She was Ojibwa from Onigaming, a reserve in Northwestern Ontario, and became a pupil at St. Mary's Residential School.

You hear of other countries. The boundaries between them. The US pullout of Iraq. Letting in ISIS and the rebels. Russia supporting Bashar al–Assad, who cannibalizes his people and guts his country. You feel fury at the world. You lash out. You are a nun wrapped in black with a Bible in your hand. Your thoughts travel everywhere. You are frustrated beyond prayer. You let out the Old Testament wrath.

Wail, for the day of the Lord is near. All hands will be feeble, and every man's heart will melt. —Isaiah 13:6–7

On the hill, the boy asks, "Is that all you have to say?" You tell him it is. Would he like to come to church? He says he would not, and drives you down from the hill, back to your house.

You see the hill where you sat in his truck when you stand in a corner of the yard. You think of his truck where you want to be, though it rattles on the road.

This is the sound of your voice. Bark. Bark.

It is time that moves forward and back with your thoughts. The soldiers and wagons. The priests with their little trilobites, the nuns. Your people crowded into reservations and boarding schools.

Behold the day of the Lord comes, cruel, with wrath and fierce anger, to make the earth a desolation. —Isaiah 13:9

Sister St. John. Did you hope for another place, but were denied by the holy fathers of the church? Did you name yourself after St. John who sat on Patmos in his exile and saw visions of the destruction to come? Is your little heart a bog of fever? Your body of bag of knucklebones? How did you sleep with the crucifix over your head? Did you want the children to know the beating Christ suffered before he went to the cross? Did you want them to feel his nails in their hands and feet? His broken teeth?

These fragments that come

Your mother was sewing in a chair, and the buttons were spread on the wide arm of the chair. You picked one of them up and put it in your mouth and couldn't breathe. She picked you up by your ankles and pounded on your back. This is the sound of her pounding. Thwak. Thwak. Until the button fell to the floor. And you breathed.

These fragments that come

You wore brown oxford shoes. You saw the boy look at them. You wanted to hide your feet.

These fragments that come

What made Sister St. John violent?

Was her head whammed against the wall? Was she hit as a child? This is the sound of someone beating. Thud. Thud. Did she study torture? Did she know firsthand the broken bones and broken teeth? Did the Germans consult her during World War II for their gas chambers?

Did terrorists?

This is the sound you will make. Ahhhh. Ahhhh. Ahhhh.

You could hang on the sash of your plaid school dress. Your mother made it long enough.

These fragments that come

The history of the button began in Pakistan [2600–1900 BCE]. Mostly a decoration, but later became something that secures two pieces of fabric together. The word *button* is French, either from *bouton* [bud] or *bouter* [push]. The first button-maker's guild was in France [1250 CE]. The dog's nose is a wet button. What else holds two things together? Plains Indian women sewing elk teeth on their buckskin dresses.

What was that dog's name? Sometimes it rode in the truck bed, its nose a button to the wind.

The boy had his arm across the back of the seat. His hand touched your shoulder. You continued to look from the hill. A car on the road. Another truck. You knew who they were. Your eyes followed them until they turned into their places. Maybe returning from the grocers or from errands in town. The sun was open. A cloud hung from a tree. He drove you back down from the hill.

A button is made of bone, horn, bronze, wood, stone, shell, metal, glass, ceramic, plastic.

What is the history of thread?

How to hold your horses

You watched the boy drive away from your place. You listened to the last sound of his truck on the road. You stood in your yard alone.

You knew the world was not yours. You knew it would be a long time before he came back. You knew he might not come back.

You were made for a family of others, but the others were scattered. Dispersed to different places. *Sheep with no one to gather them—Isaiah 13:14.*

These fragments that come

Now you find the road. You have a car. The key to it. You have a map of places you travel. You drive the plains and sleep in rest areas at night to hear the buffalo in the motors of the eighteen-wheelers lined up in their rows.

You buy gasoline. You have learned to speak. You say, "Cheeseburger to go." You only want to keep moving. The passing land is a story. Not staying where it was. You see the moving landscape moving. You find the past moving with the moving land. You drive until you feel the old wounds. You drive until you break.

Three rocks tell their stories

You find rocks at the Banff Centre in Alberta. [1] A gray rock covered with white wears a winter coat.

[2] Another rock calls to you from the path. You go back to look for it. It is the boy at the wheel of the truck with his arm across the back of the seat. You have several thoughts wandering in your head. You tell them to stay in order. Bark. Bark. They do not listen. [3] The third rock swirls with a snowstorm. By afternoon the snow's melted.

Maybe the lines in the rocks are the scars your father bore. The stories he did not tell. You are that shadow of the past from which you come.

All you have is your video camera and the moving landscape.

From the window at Banff in the northern Rockies, the nodding branches of the fir trees. The yellow flutter of cottonwoods. You are surrounded by the stories. There hardly is room on the path for you to walk.

The larger world moves around you. You are part of it, though it doesn't know you. You are invisible as a nun who had no part in the making of children, but harmed the unruly ones.

You hear the rocks speak their own language. In your cruelty you do not let them speak their words. You hit the rocks if they speak. They are small. They fly across the room. Little sections break off. They are injured. They will remember their injuries all their lives.

On the news, you see refugees from Syria looking for places to go to countries who do not want them. The refugees cannot return to the rubble of their land.

They are drowning as they cross the water. They are hungry, tired, dispirited as they stand before the barriers that have been put up. The refugees are removed from where they were. They have come unbuttoned.

For Aylan Kurdi, a three-year-old boy from Syria whose body was found on the coast of Turkey

You return to the United States from the Banff Centre, driving eighteen hundred miles. You are alone on the road with your small video camera. You think of your father. The destruction of his hope. He tried to speak his voice. But was shut down. Closed up.

It is the history of sewing.

The history of the cruelty of the world.

Card–to remove the dirt and detritus from wool and separate it into strands for weaving

You went far away to a place where no one would find you. You left bread crumbs. No, that was the story your mother told. Now it is a birdman who flew where he wanted. You wanted wings also. They became the wheels of your car.

You have boxes of cassettes in your house. Inside them, the moving land moves with the miles you have driven. You think of the thousands of miles inside the cassettes in your closet where you keep your winter coat.

You continue to film while driving back from the Banff Centre. You drive and drive.

You are the first of your father. The last of his kind. Though he is gone, you feel him with you when you travel. You have outlasted all of them, but it does not mean you are alone.

You hear the old stories again on a strange road at night as you stop from travel.

At dawn, when you drive again, you see the shadow of your car has left the car to run beside you. You film the image of your car following in the hedge grass, the embankments, the fields farther away.

PART VI

ACTS OF DISENFRAN- CHISEMENT

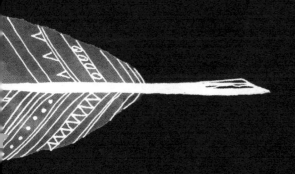

THE ARRIVAL OF RELIGION

Blind faith relies on an obedience that verges
on boredom.

—Mary Jo Bang, "The Earthquake in This Case Was"

Here it comes . . . one more churchcurdled hymn
we don't so much sing as haunt.

—Christian Wiman, The Preacher Addresses the Seminarians

I believe there is something better in it than the way the
white man acts.

—"Tushpa Crosses the Mississippi," Native American Testimony:
An Anthology of Indian and White Relations,
edited by Peter Nabakov

In an old photograph album, we were dressed for church. My father and brother in suits. My mother and I in our dresses with hats and gloves. Sometimes, we went out to eat after church. It was a family activity. It was significant. Boringly significant. It was only one day a week. I could go to school and play after school, the next. We were decent. And American. We were bedrock.

We lived in desperation. The parents pulled in different ways. Yet they stuck together with the glue of work and house and church and children who went to school.

I am shortsighted with shortcomings. It was terrible enough that Christ suffered intensely on the cross to relieve me. A relief that would come in the afterlife, toward which I struggled with desperation. How could all that be boring? But it was. It was.

Sometimes I thought of other things in church. I looked at the architecture. The stained window glass that depicted Biblical characters on their own journeys. Probably far more boring with long days and longer nights. Without television or movies. Without the abounding grace of flannelgraphs.

I woke one morning, dreaming a boy in the next house was being eaten by a tiger. I heard his screams. Instead of running to help, I stayed in my own house. I would not fight tigers, though David did. I would save my own life.

Depression probably is the word I am looking for. A spiritual depression. I believe God is. I believe Christ is. I believe the Holy Ghost is. I belong to them by faith. It is like a long journey by car.

At least I don't walk through the desert or ride a donkey or camel. I have my own car. I know how to cut through Kansas and drive to California in two days. Less than two days. I always had daylight once I got there. Unless winter. I remember once wanting to flee church so bad I shook.

But I stayed. I have always stayed. I always will stay. I belong to Christ. I believe within the gospel is everlasting life. The missionaries came with soldiers to teach us this and to rid us of the desperate attacks of panic.

"The missionaries arrived in our country along the California coast with a small troop. . . . The Fernandino Father remains in our country with the little troop that he brought." —Pablo Tac, a Luiseno Indian, 1822.

The Indians carried stones from the sea for foundations for the missions, to make bricks, roof tiles, to cut beams, reeds, and what was necessary. "The Fernandino Father, as he was alone and . . . seeing it would be very difficult for him alone to give orders to that people" always had the little military troop with him.

"Tomorrow the sowing begins and so the laborers go to the chicken yard to assemble."

I'm not sure those are the right words, but it is what I copied down, and I like the disconnect. Sometimes language is a shifting terrain.

When I was in California, I thought I would visit the missions built northward along the California coast. One weekend, I traveled to the closest one, San Buenaventura. There were people and crowds and traffic. Most of the day was spent getting there and back.

San Diego de Alcala, 1769
San Carlos Borromeo Carmelo, 1770
San Antonio de Padua, 1771

San Gabriel Arcangel, 1771
San Luis Obispo de Toloso, 1772
San Francisco de Asis, 1776
San Buenaventura, 1782
Santa Barbara, 1786
La Purisima Concepcion, 1787
Santa Cruz, 1791
Neustra Senora de la Soledad, 1791
San Jose, 1797
San Juan Bautista, 1797
San Miguel Arcangel, 1797
San Fernando Rey di Espana, 1798
Santa Ines, 1817
San Francisco Solano, 1823

Often, religion is irritating. How can something that I consider at stake be diminished as it often is on Sundays? The old hymns. The new jumping, jived-up worship service with drums so loud they vibrate in my chest. In fact, the drummer is behind Plexiglas to deflect some of the noise. Sometimes the stage lights twirl. The minister is reeved.

There are times the tedium is an excabator. A word my young grandson called the excavator. He loved the large construction trucks and machinery. I don't have the right word either, but it defines the wrongness I feel I get from religious services that try so hard.

ACTS OF DISENFRANCHISEMENT

I need faith. I need the righteousness of Christ I lack when I am revealed to myself in all my desolation. The dizzingly boring services. The habit of going. Of Sunday morning on the pew listening to hymns I cannot sing.

What do songs mean to me anyway, written two hundred years ago? The pokey organ. The sameness of the service. The sermon consisting of what thought the pastor came up with during the week. A leading of the Holy Ghost through the tedium. The same road. Over and over.

Yet I attend. I always have attended. I always will attend. Now it is Sunday morning. I go to church. It is a small indication of the enormity of heaven and my movement toward it.

THE DOME OF HEAVEN

Making an Independent Film I Have Wanted to Make

A Retrospect

Dreams are dangerous. They uncover your bones. They bleed you. Dreams are a swarm of insects I remember on a summer evening moving over the yard. They fly independent of one another, yet belong together as a group. Their cohesiveness is in their brokenness hovering on the edge of darkness and back.

My Aunt Martha Petithory has died. I divide her estate between the six nephews and nieces. I receive a portion. Not enough to make the independent film I have wanted to make, but to start. To get into it. She was an I-shall-not-be-moved Christian. She and Uncle Lou had no children. They lived a quiet, sparing life. That was her word—we must be sparing. The dining room furniture they had all their lives had been his mother's. They were married over fifty years when Uncle Lou died. They would not approve of an independent film. I can hear them say, "Do not use our money for this."

But I have a dream. A vision.

Now I am thinking how to get into this. Off the gutter on the porch, drips of rain fall on large, wet leaves like the snap of fingers—or like a rock in the tire tread that makes a steady snap when the car is on the road. I begin to feel a rhythm. There's an energy coming. Something is going to happen if I can step into it.

Everywhere I go, I think about how to do this. I wake at 3:00 in the morning. What am I doing? What has caused me to do this? I don't know how to make a film. I don't know how to direct. There are other places that need the money. That I need the money. Where did this dream come from? Senility at the end of my life? A wrong turn into the grandiose? Impracticality? But in the psalms, as elsewhere in the Bible, which I read in my stress, I find the impossible accomplished.

So much against it. Funding, funding, and funding are the components of filmmaking. But things begin to fall into place. People are willing to act in it. People are willing to donate. I purchase insurance. Consider the budget. I still wake with the mystery of how it will be met.

I am needy—I am needy—Psalm 109:22. This is the supplication of anyone making a film.

I read *Conquest of the Useless: The Making of the Fitzcarraldo*, by Werner Herzog, about the difficulties of filmmaking, including moving a steamboat over a steep incline to the river on the other side.

My parents and former husband would tell me I can't do it, if they were here. I know I'm up against something more than I can do. I visit my brother. "Do it before you won't be able to," he says. "Do it while you still can." Do it before before I forget which side of the road to drive on.

In November 2009, one month before filming, I am on my way to Vici, Oklahoma, to find locations. I-35 south from Kansas City, then west across Oklahoma. Usually an eight-hour trip. Along the road, I see the hedge apples in a tree like a flock of birds in its branches. They are that same swarm formation I remember in the insects.

I decide December 7–14, 2009, we will shoot what we can. One actor has to leave the fifteenth. Another actor had to leave the sixteenth. Another can't arrive until after the seventh. Another can't arrive until late on the eighth. The airport in Oklahoma City is three hours away. That is six hours for whoever picks them up. I don't have drivers. I don't have a camera crew. I return to Kansas City, then drive to Vici, Oklahoma, again. The Dewey County sheriff and the assistant district court judge agree to be in the film. The Vici high school principal says I can film there. The public relations officer at Southwestern Oklahoma State University in Weatherford says I can film there. I visit the Vici nursing home to ask if I can use a room for Franklin's hospital scene. It is pouring rain. They agree. I visit the Vici Restaurant and ask if they can provide meals in their backroom. They can—chicken fried steak or chicken fried chicken. Housing is more difficult. There are no motels in Vici. The closest ones are thirty minutes away in Seiling and Woodward.

What if it snows? What if it's overcast while we are there? I think of all the lovely days that have passed since I have wanted to make this film. Now I get into it again at the last part of the year, probably the worst time to make a film.

In Weatherford, Oklahoma, I stand at a fence on the north end of Seventh Street, looking back toward Vici, where Flutie wants to run from college. I stand there at the rusted gate before I feel her with me— before I feel the rusted fields of Oklahoma's red soil in the distance. I see the wind bending the row of weeds by the fence, hissing through a gnarled tree and the spruce bush.

I leave Oklahoma in the afternoon to drive back to Kansas City again—some eight hours away. The sandy roads seem like hands that pull at the car. I hurry over the wettest places to get through them. I see the return of clouds on the western horizon. The prospect of filmmaking is getting sucked into the wet, sandy soil of the road. But I wake mornings seeing the scenes and hearing dialogue.

When evening came, the boat was out on the sea, and he was alone on the land. When he saw that they were straining at the oars against an adverse wind, he came towards them early in the morning, walking on the sea. He intended to pass them by. But when they saw him walking on the sea, they thought it was a ghost and cried out; for they all saw him and were terrified. But immediately he spoke to them and said, "Take heart, it is I; do not be afraid." —Mark 6:47–50

Filmmaking is a stroll on the sea. Filmmaking is a calling out.

What are you looking for? What do you want?— Jesus asked in John 1:3. I want to make a film. I want to go to Vici, Oklahoma, with $40,000 of my own money and another $20,000 in donations and savings, and make a film that will cost at least three times what I have.

I had been in contact with the Screen Actors Guild because I wanted to use five of their actors. SAG emailed me a low-budget contract. Thirty-nine pages. The printer ran out of ink before it all printed. I can't handle this, I emailed back. They sent an ultralow budget contract. I signed it and returned it to the agents.

How could I tell this group I returned from LA to Kansas City in two days? Fourteen hours each day. These hidden things I have known in secret. They can't be blurted out. But they are the reason I think I can do this.

The film is based on the myth of Philomela, whose brother-in-law raped her and cut out her tongue so she couldn't tell. She wove a tapestry of the event and sent it to her sister, who knew then what happened. The sister cut up their son, fed the pieces to her husband, and fled. When he followed then, the women turned into birds and flew away.

Sometimes you build on a story already told. Rape is not an issue in the film, but the inability to speak is. The story of Philomela wrestles a story from silence. It makes silence speak. The need to tell our story. The myth of Philomela became a road map through the film, as Flutie began to speak from her silence.

Once, on my way to Oklahoma on I-35, I stopped to film a field full of hay rolls. A red-tailed hawk flew to the fence post right in front of me. It sat there until the noise of an approaching truck made it fly away. It is the tailpiece of the film.

On the last day of November 2009, one week before I want to start filming, still without a crew, I drive to Lawrence, Kansas. The man I talk to says they can't get ready that fast. I keep talking until I have a camera crew. They will arrive in Vici on December 7, 2009.

After the first few days of filming, he later told me, the crew had a bet they would have to pack up and return to Lawrence. But we didn't abandon the film.

I rent a four-bedroom house outside Vici where I stay. The first night, a cow breaks the wellhead. We are without water. There are five of us in the house. I wake at 4:00 in the morning. It is below freezing. I hear sleet against the windows.

The next day, at a house in the country, the second one I rent, the toilet won't work. I rent a portable one, which they set in the front yard while we are gone for lunch. It is bitter cold. Zero degrees with a wind chill below zero as we stand in the yard. Now a mower we need for a scene won't start—Now there is not time to finish shooting the scheduled scenes before dark.

Each day, I ask, what disaster will it be today? But each day, there also was a magic. We shot until December 14 when I packed up. I took one actor to Norman, Oklahoma, to visit a friend who would take him to the Oklahoma City airport the next day. I drive eight hours back to Kansas City in the dark.

There were a few cold nights in Vici when the sky was clear. We stood in the yard in the dark, looking at the canopy of stars over us. Not even a yard light to hide the sky from the open land that disappeared into nothingness until we were standing in the constellations. I remember once raising my hand as if touching their pavilion.

We returned for the second and last week of filming, April 11–16, 2010. This time, it was the wind that was the weather. I remember, after the cemetery scene, helping a lady with a cane back to the car. Each day, there was forecast for possible rain. Heavy clouds passed, but rain did not fall the first four days of the week. On Friday, the clouds opened. Rain fell the entire day.

The last night of filming, the cast and crew went to a café in Seiling to eat and celebrate. I went back to the house to pack because, once again, I had to take one of the actors to the Oklahoma City airport the next morning for a 7:30 flight. I was crying anyway. Filming was over. What was the matter? It was the absolute relief I felt.

I remembered that I had plane tickets for the actors before I had the film crew. I thought of the disasters that could have happened.

I think part of the trauma I felt afterward was from the realization that I had been through a war. A war on a minute scale, of course. I felt the weight of the heavy task of filmmaking. There wasn't the satisfaction of finishing a book. But a near disaster, as if I had touched something bigger than myself, and somehow it had not devoured me.

The process of filmmaking had accessed the wounded, the hurt and hidden places in me, something like driving long distances on the highway.

And yet, filmmaking is a parade. It is an accumulation of floats and, at the same time, a deconstruction of form. The air is full of flying confetti. The parade is a band of moving objects. They are only fragments.

I had to borrow money to meet the payroll the first week. I visited the banker. I had funds, I said. But it would take too long to roll them over. I don't have my tax refund yet. I received a loan of $15,000.

Later, I read Orhan Pamuk's *The Museum of Innocence*: "Meanwhile, Feridun had begun to resemble the directors one heard about. The chaotic speed of filming having robbed him of his childish air, in two months it was as if he'd aged ten years" [Chapter 67, "Cologne"].

"He [Feridun, the director] took on the air of a soldier just returned from a long and disastrous campaign" [Chapter 70, "Broken Lives"].

As it turned out, the editing of the film continued the struggle. It felt like a multitude of puzzle parts all out of order, floating loose in the air. I had an editor. I made trips to Lawrence, Kansas, over the next three months to watch him work. We'd had to cut many scenes from the script because of funding. During filming, I had stayed up late at night, working out the budget. I had gotten up early, while it was still dark, to write scenes to bridge those we had to leave out. During editing, it was hard to piece the story together, but he did it.

Also, Flutie's story was my story and a composite of many students I had over the years, mainly when I worked for the State Arts Council of Oklahoma in the 1980s. Now, seeing the story once again before my eyes, it brought up hurt I had buried, like salt water from the underground ocean that is mentioned in the film. On the edge of Vici, there's an iodine plant that extracts the salt water. You can smell the underground ocean when you pass.

The film is about struggle. "Everything is hard. Nothing is easy," Flutie's father says toward the end of the film.

We had a screening of the film in the Vici high school auditorium. I could not have made the film without the townspeople. The Randalls provided the soundtrack. They acted in the film. The Vici banker drove to Pittsburg, Kansas, for a 1940 Ford coupe. When I needed a red dress for Geneva's wedding, I had five dresses to choose from by afternoon. In a town of just over seven hundred people. Whatever was needed, the people there provided.

After the June 22 screening, I was depressed when I left Vici the next morning. I'm not sure why. As I drove through the Glass Mountains, they sparkled in the sun. It was a shot I had wanted in the film, but the camera crew couldn't get it because of rain.

I kept driving.

Whose feet they hurt with fetters; he was laid in iron—Psalm 105:18. The sidenotes in one of the translations about this text and Joseph in prison in Egypt says, "His soul came into iron." That's what I felt. My soul caught in iron. If I just held on, as Joseph held on in prison in the story of the book of Exodus, there would be a change.

That is the purpose of writing—and making film—to set free these places that have been held in captivity within me, within us.

FOUR QUARTERS

*Which of you, intending to build a tower, does not first
sit down, and count the cost?*

—Luke 14:28

Some years ago, I drove to Death Valley on my way
from southern California to Kansas after a Native
Voices program. When I can, I like to take out-of-the-
way journeys during my travels because I pick up voices
from the land.

I took some footage on the trip with my Sony
Handycam because I knew by then, my next independent film would come from Death Valley. It was
where the land spoke the story to me. The film would
be about two young Timbisha Shoshoni men, Burris and Bucky, and their struggle with distance from
self and community after they left Furnace Creek for
college. Disenfranchisement is a common theme in
Native literature. *Four Quarters* is about the impact of
education on Native culture. The academic Indian is
now another disenfranchisement in the mix.

Four quarters, the four directions. It is the point
or concept that holds oppositions together. The
extremes of north and south. The differences of east
and west. The extremes of internal weather. A moral

and spiritual compass. Shortcomings and strengths. The components of debts and assets. The point that holds our internal directions in balance.

Several years ago, at the National Museum of the American Indian in Washington, DC, I saw the Fritz Scholder exhibit. There was one particular painting of Scholder's, *Four Indian Riders*—in which three horsemen stand together, with a fourth in the shadows on a plain of bright yellow grass. It's where I got the idea to block the script into four parts. It's where I got the idea to pursue a shadowy character—the Native scholar. I wanted Burris and Bucky to show what is gained and what is lost in these recent positions for Indians on college and university campuses.

To live in this world, we have to be educated, but to become educated, we lose part of ourselves. That distance also has been my life experience. It is what I wanted to present in Four Quarters. There also was a question I wanted to ask: What imprint does the American educational system make on a traditional culture?

As soon as the semester was up in December 2013, and I had turned in my grades at Azusa Pacific University, I started for the Viejas Reservations just east of San Diego on I-80 with six actors and seven of the crew. We filmed over the next four days.

In the first act, *Runage*, Burris and Bucky travel from LA to a conference. When Burris's Volvo has trouble, they call a towing company run by traditional Indians.

Burris and Bucky come face to face with the distance between themselves and their past. While on the road, they also hear about the death of their old friend, Ralph, in Furnace Creek, Death Valley.

In the second act, Senior Scorpion, Senior Fish, Burris and Bucky meet at In Jun's Café in LA where they debate a trip back to Death Valley to reconnect with their roots, and to visit Ralph's grave. In the café, with its trendy Native American decor, they face the facsimile of their constructed world.

In the third act, 8 Ball, Keelee, Burris's wife, and Yerma, Bucky's sometimes girlfriend, meet two other friends for dinner. Yerma hears that Bucky and Burris plan a trip back to Furnace Creek.

In the fourth act, Four Quarters, Burris and Bucky travel from LA back to Furnace Creek with Keelee and Yerma to visit the arbor on a cliff above Furnace Creek. They visit their high school and make a stop at Ralph's grave and also their parents' graves in the cemetery.

Filming was another act of disenfranchisement. On the Viejas Reservation, several hundred miles south of Death Valley. A different terrain.

I listened to reason instead of my vision. I let myself be persuaded. Death Valley was too remote. But as we filmed, and later, as I drove to Death Valley Junction with a photographer to add more footage to the film, it was where we should have filmed.

I like the questions in the film. Where are we? Do we ever leave where we're from? Do we ever find our way back? The film ends with a question that had been buried elsewhere in the script. Bucky: "What do you do with wounds that won't heal?" Keelee: "You keep licking them."

At one time, I had a small cabin with a small dock and ramp on the Lake of the Ozarks in Missouri. When I had to replace the dock and ramp, there was trouble aligning the new ramp and dock with the foundation block on the shore. Up the road, some men were clearing brush from a ditch. The tractor was borrowed, and the block moved to line up with the new ramp and dock. But the foundation stone had been broken from its base, and the dock soon pulled the block farther off its base. I had it reinforced, but it kept moving farther away from its place.

A metaphor for the characters in *Four Quarters* who had been pulled from their foundation and broken from their past.

What do you do when all you have is a script and somewhere around $25,000, which is a fraction of what it takes to film? Less than a crumb.

You leave the characters in their chairs in a minimalistic world of dialogue.

You leave them in their car moving slowly over a Viejas Reservation road. A camera mounted on its hood.

You make the film anyway.

WHY THE ROCKS
HAVE EARS

*Joshua took a great stone and set it under an oak by
the sanctuary of the Lord, and said, this stone will be a
witness for us for it has heard all the words of the Lord he
spoke to us.*

—Joshua 24:26–27

We have something between us that cannot be spoken.
If it is, it will drown us. But we are not in a boat, but in
the desert. Traveling. Separately.

As this is the first drop of a stone into the water.
Or the water onto stone. I want to get into the crev-
ices. The jelly roll. The roly-polys that curve back
into themselves when you pick them up.

When something cannot be spoken, it is there.
Eventually.

I had my bungalow in Kansas painted while I
was in California. I didn't pick the sheen. It is shiny,
nearly white. An iceberg. A glacier.

I think of the mistakes I have made.

Now there comes on illness.

Now it is past.

The Native culture is based on oral tradition. At the center of its structure is an energy field that is a spider spinning its web, radiating outward from the core, catching the rays of the sun, implicating the enormity of the solar system in a few small strands. We are the smallness of creation in proportion to the universe, yet we carry an enormity within us, or part of it, or a similitude of it. This pattern of the large within the small. This pattern in the small carries an implication of the large.

It is the web that holds the rocks together.

I am by myself on a trip west, when I stop at petroglyphs along the highway. There is a slowing of moving. A going that halts. A struggle to stop when the driving wants to keep going. Exit 187 off I-70 onto 94—a dirt road three miles north into a dead-end canyon. It was the Utes here. In the heat. Making marks on rocks by scratching with a smaller rock or animal bone in 600–1250 CE. Somehow related to the Anasazi at Mesa Verde. The Fremont people in Utah, a marker explains. The name, Fremont, from John Fremont, a mid-nineteenth-century explorer and surveyor who made note of the figures he found.

The figures are a story in which the message is not clear. They are strange triangular figures—ghostlike, with horns and missing eyes, missing arms and legs. They are part of the Barrier Canyon–style petroglyphs found also in the plateaus of Colorado, Utah, and Arizona.

They were ones who came from a distance.

They were antlered-people-not-of-us.

They were those-who-were-here-in-some-form-different-than-we-know.

The winged people. The haloed ones. The horned ones.

They were visions from the outer world.

The-way-they-looked-to-each-other-in-ceremony.

The documentation of what was to them we do not know.

These large standing rocks in the canyon, themselves painted with shadows of huge white clouds over the buttes. They also bear the marking of weathering. A mark of having been a long time.

Maybe the petroglyphs are meant to pull attention upward to the night sky and the moving stars. Maybe they draw lines around certain formations they see, as we draw lines around the stars for constellations. Like Orion's belt.

This Sego Canyon rock art.

Were they shadowy figures that moved in nightmares?

Aliens from a different world?

Or in ceremonial costumes?

A child's drawings of ghosts?

Triangular bodies at an intersection of worlds?

The declarations of an unknown origin?

Or maybe the figures on the rocks are shadows of their bodies ahead of them at evening. Maybe they drew their shadows elongated on the land in the late sun that makes long shadows. Everyone knows it, walking with the sun at their back.

Long ago, I was given a professorship. After many years, I was then given retirement. I had a driver's license. I bought gasoline. I traveled alone to the west.

In travel, I knew the passing land. At first, I didn't want it to stop. But there is the necessary stoppage of travel. A destabilization of momentum. To see what is in the passing is the purpose that travel makes known. In travel, I became visible. I name it. Stone it. Shadow it.

The petroglyphs are flying. They are arriving. The cliff behind them reaches the lines and fragments of strata. Only when I am awake at night. I think their forms move.

I made him mad—my son-in-law. I said what I knew until I was vernalized. [I should not say everything I think.] Now there is that between us. As if there wasn't enough already. And I am pushed farther away. I should get used to the wilderness. I should find the beasts that live there.

We are in the world together, but we are of different worlds. We have discovered our separation. It is his world that is up now. I step back. Away. Though I am not ready to step. It is my place too. It is the ceremony I must follow west. This is the ghost dance of what is actual. The brutal going on of life. The survival of them. Their way of it. It is theirs.

In the old days, the mother-in-law wore bells so he would know she was coming. They could not be there together.

And what should I do with knowledge? Stain it? Mark a ceremony of it? That is the work of the petroglyph.

There are noises in the house.

Their portals are knives. Their door posts and lintels.

He does not know he is in the desert. That is his mistake. Do not tell him. The knowledge is somewhere in his closet. He will pull it down someday.

We carry within us our own demise. Mostly.

Gradually, though, we come to know the coded messages.

The petroglyphs are the same in different parts of the world. This primitive form of the human being made visible in subtle movement across continents. Just as the child curls up his tongue as he works with fervor on his drawing. His characters are like petroglyphs. They relate the primitive brain as it came up from the past. Yet these glyphs. These likenesses of form and structure found across the world survive.

Maybe they are archetypal symbols. Or how our vision is wired.

Some of the petroglyphs—the ones that are a series of lines instead of figures—may have been maps. Showing migration trails and places water could be found. Those are the circles. The spirals. A mnemonic of how to get there.

Maybe the petroglyphs are from hallucinogens they used in ceremony. Here comes Uncle Roth from behind the rock. See how strange he looks.

The petroglyphs seem to come out of the rock.

I traveled once in heavy fog. The ordinary world was not found there. Only the black soil of a plowed field. A dark outline of hedgerows. A herd of angus that seemed to levitate as if petroglyphs on rock facing. An occasional fir tree suspended in fog. Sometimes a dark farmhouse or barn in the distance.

The sky prowls in the rock. The sky was a bigger part of their lives. At night—the stars and formations, the falling stars. A sky full of stones. The moving parts of it moving. They told stories of their origins. A pool of rocks. Of water moving over rocks. Of rocks in moving water. Their stories stood out in the vapor.

You see for a moment before it disappears. The unknowable. Or yet unknown.

My car in travel once again. In different places of its versions. In different versions of its places. Unknowable as petroglyphs. As scripture. The necessary attempt of interpreting is what is driven. The different interpretations my son-in-law and I have. The picking up of moving. The struggle to continue. Until momentum is achieved. This running from a place I do not fit. The house of my leaving.

Possibly the petroglyphs leave behind what cannot be attached after breakage.

THE WRITING OF TRAVEL–THE TRAVEL OF WRITING

As he that takes away a garment in cold weather.

—*Proverbs 25:20*

Once I drove from St. George, Utah, to Kansas City in eighteen hours through snow rising in Utah and on the summit of the Rockies where traffic was stopped because of an accident.

Start into it again: Once I was in the Rockies in the snow. The trucks traveled with lights on their foreheads. There are visions in blowing snow when you are pushed into yourself, and all the journeys through the snow return when one is snow-blinded or worked-with-snow that drifts into the head, and you can't see for the blowing snow, and you can't clear out your head until you think, and, in thinking, you thought you saw something approaching—a bear or horse or another truck with lights on its forehead.

You bear your visions in cold, which could tear your fingers off and blacken your toes. You wish for comfort. You wish not to be cold. But you are walking with those who walked through the snow, though you are stopped in a line of traffic as far as you can see on I-70 through the Rockies on an incline, and the snow is beautiful if only you weren't stuck in it. Or those broken down or just broken in their circumstances and over it you hear the Earth and maybe the whole sky crying because it is lost, and the snow is the grieving you receive on your windshield. You use the wipers to push it aside, and a residue of road-dirt smudge moves over your windshield, trying to obscure your vision or even part of your vision to make it more difficult. It waits to pounce on you with its heavy weight because you are traveling alone, as you always do, because no one wants to go with you where you go. Or you don't want them to go. It is better to travel alone. You don't have to listen to anyone but the past that speaks in the silent snow.

Even all the snow fences in Wyoming to the north can't hold it back.

The book of Hosea and all those dismal prophets are a drive through the mountains. Like a leopard by the way I will observe them—Hosea 13:7. It comes to me as a vision—the cold. A leopard. Eyes of fire. Teeth of ice. A snow leopard sitting on the mountain. The spirit over our land.

You see the shadow of the mountains as if they were men.
                                                    —Judges 9:36

And where do stories come from after all? What vast plain the imagination? Out of desperation? A struggle to show chaos that language is chief?

What is it in the old Indian wars that covered the tribes even before the coming of the Europeans? Not the words but the meaning underneath that can't be gotten to—but only pointed the way. The fears and longings for solutions. The nothingness that waits on each side of the road.

Maybe stories are what did not happen, but maybe on some distant plain, some reading somewhere, passage after passage without a map. Maybe stories are a way to make a map.

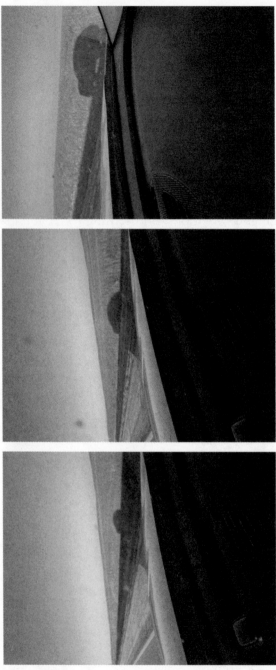

The shadow of the car was taken by Diane Glancy on her iPhone, I-35 in the Foothills of Kansas.

ROUGH FOOTAGE

In the beginning of the world
there was a car driving on the road.
There was darkness.
When light came the shadow of the car
ran beside the car.
The shadow thought it was its own being
independent of its object.
The car called the shadow back
but the shadow ran and ran
until light went away.
There is the sound of a car running with its shadow.
There is the shadow running beside the car
silent as those petroglyphs on desert rocks
are silent as the objects they shadowed
in the beginning of the world.

PART VII

A MOVING
POINT OF
REFERENCE

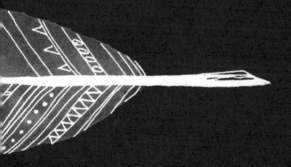

A MOVING POINT
OF REFERENCE

He compassed me with gall and travel.

—*Lamentations 3:5*

Memory is a moving point of reference. A centering from one's own mapping. Memory runs like an internal file. A compass in which the directions point to the directions the rememberer wants to remember. There are hard points of truth somewhere in the variables.

I am driving to San Francisco. I park and sleep in the Walmart parking lot with cars and campers and RVs. The wallpaper of the journey. The passing landscape. The train in the desert with its railcars like large shoeboxes on wheels.

My cousin's daughter is getting married. The granddaughter of my aunt—the one I found waiting at the front door when I visited her, the one who said she was waiting for her parents to arrive from the farm, who learned to swim in the coalpits near Hume, Missouri, when she was a girl. The one who lived a few months short of her one hundredth birthday.

I drive 1,972 miles from Gainesville, Texas, to San Francisco in a new car I am not used to.

Midway across Utah, I leave the interstate and take Highway 50 across the rest of Utah and Nevada. I stop at the Hickison petroglyphs. Elevation, 6,564. Here, the rock work is not as distinct as in the Sego Canyon. They mostly are a series of lines on rock facings. Maybe a form of writing before writing. Or maybe another interpretation of the night sky.

I smell the pinyon pines and hear the wind in the junipers from the enormous emptiness across the valleys.

East of Reno on Highway 50, I see a haze. I began to smell smoke. On the car radio, I hear about the forest fire in northeast California along I-80, about sixty miles from Sacramento. The strong easterly wind carries the smoke into the Nevada desert. The fire would burn over ninety-seven thousand acres before it was contained.

The inspection-station guards at the California border wore masks. I held a damp hand towel to my nose as I drove. Thick smoke for the next forty-six miles, a highway marker read. I drove on through the haze to Sacramento for the night.

When I saw a grid of power lines in California, I remembered the Hickison petroglyphs. I remembered them again when I saw the lines of a few stray clouds at dusk, and the cluster of stars that would begin to shine.

A MOVING POINT OF REFERENCE

The Museum of Modern Art in New York City ignored Native American petroglyphs and pictographs in an exhibit.

—*Colonizing Abstraction: MoMA's Inventing Abstraction Show Denies Its Ancient Global Origins*, G. Roger Denson, Cultural Critic, the Blog, January 23, 2014

SHOEBOX

A Story that Bears a Similitude to Likeness

[or the story retold that is the same story and yet nothing like it]
Accept this truth as fiction.
It is the reason I can't stay in one place too long.

We made a house from a shoebox in my parents' closet where we played the afternoons we had to pass. There were two of us. I was the child and Miss Euel the sitter of the child until I was old enough to sit by myself.

Meanwhile, we played with what we could. Cutting door and window in one of my mother's shoeboxes. Using a scrap of material for a curtain. Cut from the pocket of a dress she never wore—at least I said I never had seen my mother wear it. The too-wide hem of a dress or skirt. The material no one would know was gone from up inside the lining of a winter coat. We used lint for hair, and the people were clothespins Miss Euel found in a bottom drawer in the pantry off the kitchen.

"Mrs. Jael is here for supper," Miss Euel said. "What shall we serve?"

Butter and potatoes.

In the old days, women made butter in butter molds that stamped the butter with their own patterns.

"Did that really happen?" I asked. Did anything really happen that we were a part of? Wasn't it all a box with a lid that kept us from seeing outside?

Late in the afternoon, we put the shoes back into the box, and closed the shutters of the windows, and put the door we cut toward the back wall of the closet so my mother wouldn't see it until she took down the box, and maybe she would only see the shoes she took from the box, and not the windows and door we cut, and the spot of glue where the curtains had been.

We were giddy with the making of our own world. If my mother was one who noticed anything, she would have seen the cuts.

My father's two-toned car lounged across the road when we took Miss Euel home. The thick rows of houses. The single church. But she would be back. Wasn't it written somewhere? Wasn't it on the schedule forever? Wasn't she booked?

The lid of a box was something to place over the space inside the box, Miss Euel told me the afternoons we played. It was a rectangle—a shape longer than it was wide. It was the space of a body with its legs together and its arms folded over its chest.

Sometimes we played Bible stories with the clothes-pins, wrapping them in robes. Placing them in a desert tent we made from the shoebox. Often we played Jael and Sisera—Jael being the woman who hammered Sisera's head to the ground with a tent stake.[1]

Once in the attic, Miss Euel and I found a fold-ed-up tent. Cast iron skillet. Coleman lamp and stove. Metal knives and forks. Nothing anyone would miss. Folding saw. Ground cloth. Tent stakes and hammer.

"When had we camped?" Miss Euel asked.

I didn't know. Before I was old enough to remem-ber. Maybe my father went hunting. Maybe it was where they went while they still had my brother. The older brother with wide eyes that saw the inside of water as if it were a box.

Sometimes we played camping with the shoebox.

"My folding saw," I said, picking up the small, metal utensil. "My hammer." I said—and beat the clothespins until they cracked.

"Just like your father," Miss Euel said.

I felt he knew what was going on in the little house of my head. My father with his ear to the window of my thinking. I was stamped with his pattern.

"Undress the clothespins. Put them back in the pantry drawer," Miss Euel said when it was time for my father to return. I hid the scraps of fabric—ate the lint. "Leave the clothespins in a heap," I said to her. "Don't rescue any of them."

---

1   Judges 5:25–26.

HOELUN

She had been at home without her hat [headdress] and
without her hat she followed their trail.

—*The Secret History of the Mongol Queens*, Jack Weatherford

A swift dromedary traversing her ways.

—Jeremiah 2:23

The heavy burden. The long overland journey in a
wagon jumping over the uneven land. Hoelun [the
mother of Genghis Kahn], in her cart pulled by yak
or ox, traveled at night in the twelfth century. The
onward going. The momentum of travel. Of getting
somewhere through the desolation of the land that is
desert after desert.

It was the pattern of the journey. The classes I
had to teach. The classes I wanted to teach. To sit at
a small liberal arts college with twelve or fifteen students. To posit a thought. To see what they said. The
going around. The carts decorated in their various
ways were the papers they handed in. The panel presentations. Their variations. The woven patterns of
blankets and coverings. The sweat of animals.

Resilience and initiative. When I look back,
those themes separate my life from my childhood. I

stopped receiving presents from aunts and uncles. I stopped being the recipient. I was on my own. A first step toward being on my own. It was solitary. Maybe I hoped to go back. To begin again. The way ahead as an adult is taking that step, the struggle. It's in the struggle that the means of the struggle are reached.

In the dark of the night, I wish I could drive in the darkness without headlights to watch the vast stars over me. But I have to see the road.

When I was a child, my father made a cart for my two dolls. I went to the vacant lot to play for the day. It was my first road of independent travel. Wherever my father was transferred, there always was some sort of wilderness in which I played, an overgrown corner lot with twisted limbs of brush in which I made camp. I didn't know about Hoelun then, but her mantle had fallen upon me. The hunger for movement, for going, was there from the beginning.

In old photographs, my father's and uncles' cars were parked in the farmyard. Around them, the group of men talking in their wide-legged trousers of the 1940s. Their feet on the running board of their cars with a sense of achievement. Of ownership.

In his book, Weatherford says that Hoelun drove a high-stepping camel. I always thought of them walking across the desert in a long line, with bundles on their backs. Yes, they do pull carts and wagons. I found photographs online.

I need to repeat the loneliness of traveling alone as if I didn't get it the first time. In my car as my cart on wheels.

#NODAPL PROTEST, NORTH DAKOTA

Travel is important to my work.

I go places and there are stories surrounding them—

I feel a call to record—to establish what is there in the memory and experience of the land—

the voice of the land and the voices of those who lived there—

whose voices became place—

whose place became words—

which is the landscape of the written text—

Someday [somewhere], that pipe will leak.

—Ron His Horse Is Thunder, Standing Rock Sioux Reservation

Room on My Dance Card

On Sunday, October 9, 2016, I drove to North Dakota on my way from Billings, Montana, to Santa Fe, New Mexico. Probably eight hundred miles out of the way to see what was happening at the protest of the Dakota Access Pipeline under the Missouri River.

On the way to Standing Rock, I saw the pipeline already installed in western North Dakota. It's visible from the interstate. The bulldozers had shaved the land—cleared an ugly path through the fields. A narrow platform had been built on posts or legs off the ground, about waist high. The pipeline rests on that platform. It looked frail. Unprotected.

On I-94, I passed several transport trucks carrying pipe.

Of all the words I've heard from Sacred Stone Camp at Standing Rock, a simple one seems to speak the reason:

I am here because I had a dream about my people—elders, children—couldn't find drinking water. And when we came across a spout, oil came out of it.—News, a young Native woman, name not given

The Dakota Access Pipeline plans were made to carry crude oil for 1,134 miles from the Bakken oil fields near Stanley in the far northwest corner of North Dakota to oil storage units and tank farms in Patoka, a small town in south central Illinois.

The pipeline already passed tributaries to the Missouri River—the Heart River, Knife River, nearing the Cannonball in North Dakota as it approaches the Missouri. The Energy Transfer Partners planned to continue the pipeline southward across South Dakota, then east across the fields of Iowa into Illinois, meaning the pipeline would have to go under the Mississippi River also. The Iowa Utilities Board approved the pipeline to run from the northwest to the southeast corner of Iowa, crossing the Floyd,

A MOVING POINT OF REFERENCE

Little Sioux, Maple, and Raccoon Rivers, among others, and of course, on the eastern border of Iowa—the Mississippi.

Sunday night, I stayed in Bismarck, North Dakota, with sheriffs and highway patrol officers from other places. I heard the supervisors and workers talk. I heard the Dakota Access Pipeline [DAPL] security. It would be January instead of December when the pipeline under the Missouri River was completed because of delays caused by protests. The welders already had gone ahead to where work was not interrupted.

The weather will get cold. The protestors will leave, the officers said.

I sat listening to the conversations that danced around the breakfast room. I was invisible to them—not part of what they said. Not asked to dance. It is the story of the Native American. Not consulted. Ignored. Dismissed.

South of Bismarck, the next day, the exit from I-94 to Highway 1806 south to Cannonball was marked, but signs were not there past the exit. I had to stop and ask the way to the camp, some twenty-five miles south of I-94.

> The day was warm.
> The cottonwood leaves were bright yellow
> in the sun.
> On the way
> the cows were eating grass.
> They said, hey yo.
> I drove on knowing they said the way.

On Highway 1806, twenty miles south of I-94 where I turned off—there was a roadblock and checkpoint ahead, where state troopers asked my purpose. Ahead of me, a truck with a large catering trailer, or commissary, I think they are called, had to pull off the road. Other vehicles, usually pickups with trailers, were turned out of the way by military guards, if they were thought to carry food or supplies. I was allowed to go with a warning of what was happening ahead.

A line of flags from many Indian nations was flying in the air when I reached Standing Rock. There were cars, vans, trucks, tents, teepees, lean-tos. There was the circular meeting ground. There was a large structure, which was the kitchen. There was stacked wood. Portable bathrooms. Dogs and children. Women in long skirts walking places, stopping to talk. There were men who were the keepers—the guards of the camp.

Farther south was the protest site. Most of the people were there—saying, it's not a good idea to send oil under a life-giving river.

The large camp at Standing Rock was made of smaller groups of camps, each with their own names. Sacred Stone. Oceti Sakowin. Rosebud Camp. Red Warrior Camp.

"The largest gathering of tribes since Greasy Grass," I heard someone say.[2]

---

2   1876 Battle of Little Bighorn when Custer was killed.

Later in November, in the media, I saw the camp structures covered with tarp and plastic coverings against the snow. It had turned cold. The people were still there. Veterans had arrived. I could almost see back to the old villages camped along the Cannonball several hundred years ago. The smoke from the campfires. The warriors. The people of the camp.

Accusations flew everywhere. The protectors said that law enforcement used water spray in zero weather, tear gas, and rubber bullets on unarmed people. Law enforcement said it was their job to uphold the constitution against the lawbreakers. The Indians were camping without permits. They spit in the face of law enforcement. They impeded the work of Energy Transfer Partners, the corporation behind the pipeline. It was the Indians who were guilty of aggression, law enforcement said. The Red Warrior Camp had agitators from the outside. Law enforcement had evidence someone tried to make an IED.

Cannonball, by the way, was named after round rocks from a turbulent place in the river.

Was it the cavalry that named it, or the Indians who had seen too many of the balls the soldiers shot at them?

Now, it was the Indians who rolled over and over like the rocks in the Cannonball. Rolling, still, in the onslaught—not of cavalry and wagon trains—but bulldozers, road graders, excavators, other heavy equipment, armored vehicles, police cars, sheriff cars, security vehicles. Morton County, North Dakota, has all the weapons. They have armored vehicles. They have made a military zone. They have smeared the land with their pipeline path.

The Dakota Access Pipeline passes through sacred land. Medicine Rock is there. The Mandan say it is where they came into the world after a great flood.

One of the earliest depictions of the Sun Dance is John K. Bear's 1713 Winter Count of a Lakota Dance near Cannonball. The bulldozers and machinery have disrupted artifacts and burial grounds. They have crossed old wounds of infraction and transgression against Native tribes. They bring the repeat of history of stepping into what isn't theirs.

Even more troublesome is an old prophecy of water pollution.

When it comes to metal pipes—a matter of common sense—comes pipeline seepage. Pinhole leaks. Long seam-line cracks. Structural anomalies. Corrosion. Erosion. Rupture. Unforeseen happenings and complications.

I would say to the corporation—"What do you not understand about the sacredness of water and the danger the pipeline imposes?"

The Dakota Access Pipeline: a $3.7 billion project. What are the chances that Energy Transfer Partners, the corporation responsible, is going to abandon their project?

The Beginning of Indignation on an October Afternoon and Afterward Following on FB

For Chief Big Foot, December 29, 1890, and the photograph of his body in the snow with arm raised.

They come from the hill—the diesel tractors and excavators—the graders and trucks with pipes lined up on their backs. The guards have water hoses and rifles that shoot rubber bullets. The horses and Indians stand their line at the Missouri and Cannonball Rivers. They are a confluence of resistance. A sun by day. A moon in the night. Snow and wind and cold. Still, the Indians remain like cornstalks after harvest— they stand in a blizzard beside a frozen excavator in the field—its arm uplifted like one of the dead.

Even the Stones Speak

It is Native land—the 1851 and 1868 Fort Laramie Treaties say it is—still, loaders and graders uproot burial grounds and ancient sites[3]. Though not marked, they are there.

---

3   With acknowledgment to "Remembering a River: The Cannonball River in History," by Dakota Wind, Standing Rock Sioux. His entire article is on the website—https://lastrealindians.com/news/2016/10/ 18/oct-18-2016-remembering-a-river-the-cannonball- river-in-history-by-dakota-wind. His history blog: http://thefirstscout.blogspot.com.

The land is a repository of history. Meriwether Lewis and William Clark camped on the Missouri River at its tributary, the Cannonball, October 18, 1804. Clark wrote about the round "grindstones" in his journal. Other explorers followed. Then fur traders. Land surveyors. Soldiers. Miners on their way to the Black Hills. Wagon trains. Settlers.

The land marks those who pass there. In turn, the land is marked with the passing of those who pass there.

The #NoDAPL site is a place of history. Indian tribes made their encampments.

Mandan. Arikara. Dakota. Lakota. Cheyenne. There have been skirmishes between tribes. There have been deaths from floods. Dakota Goodhouse wrote that thirty lodges or some 150 to 180 people drowned in 1825. The Winter Counts of Blue Thunder, No Two Horns, and High Dog recount the flood in the wolf moon, when chunks of ice and water rose from the river. Many Mandan drowned in the Cannonball with their horses.

In 1837, Annie Skye, Hunkpapa, said that out of a clear blue sky, smallpox hit them in their encampment along the river.

In 1862, a band of Lakota fought the Cheyenne, who set fire to the plains to retaliate. Many caught in their camps were killed or burned while running to the river.

All of them interred their dead along the river. Their bones disintegrated among rock fragments and soil—through drowning, European diseases, fire, defeat, reservations, more disease, hunger, poverty, boarding schools—whatever came.

The Dakota Access Pipeline builds in seemingly noninvasive, half-acre fragments under the radar of long-haul regulations. They build in segments and do not answer for the length of their trail. The hefty tanks shovel off the grass with its roots from the ground to make an ugly path for an uglier pipeline lifted on stilts.

The pipeline route at first was planned to run north of Bismarck, where it was not wanted. Let it cross on Indian land, they must have said.

Energy Transfer Partners asked no permission. Did no environmental impact study. They saw no grave markers, no markers of sacred sites. And they moved in. Until voices at Standing Rock asked—What are you doing? Your trucks butcher the land. You endanger the river. The ancestors watch. The hawk and falcons call. The holy ones stand up. Even the wild buffalo gather. They sent their Morse-code message in grunts—Why are soldiers here again with their guns?

I drove to North Dakota in my car that uses gas and oil. I did not walk, ride a horse, or pedal a bike. No, it is oil I use to make long travels. With a pouch of tobacco and small rocks I have collected from travels, I sleep in my car, the backseat pulled down. A short suitcase on the floorboard, a pillow on top of it, to make a bed the length of the car from the back of the driver's front seat to the tailgate. My sleeping bag fits in that space in the Ford Edge. My traveling companion. My horse. Our shadows are one.

Will you be quiet?—I say to the stones I carry in my car—just for a moment. They have come from different places, like the tribes gathered at the confluence of the Cannonball and Missouri rivers with as many voices in the complexity of issues. The authorities there to uphold the law. The Indians trying to draw the authorities into doing something the Indians could publicize, authorities say. A North Dakota farmer now wears a sidearm as he drives his harvester through his alfalfa field. He said the Indians drove into his field to unload their horses. He asked them to leave. They asked him to leave.

On December 4, 2016, the headline came—"US Corps of Engineers Refused to Grant Easement for the Dakota Access Pipeline."

What had Indians done? This camp of the underestimated withstanding without weapons a $3.7 billion corporation.

A day or two later, a North Dakota blizzard hit. The subzero weather put the immediate conflicts on hold, as people looked for shelter [except those in winterized tents with heating].

The elation also was muffled in the realization that Energy Transfer Partners were not likely to back down. It was reported that Morton Country police protecting the pipeline were fewer. But if the bear cats weren't frozen [diesel fuel does not do well in the cold], ETP probably would be pushing under the Missouri River.

In another Facebook posting, some North Dakota ruffians badgered two young Native men in a van leaving the Bismarck Ramada. They blocked the Natives with their vehicles in front and behind. They stood at the windows threatening. Eventually the ruffians left, after intimidation.

For one moment, nonetheless, for one large moment, the probability and eventual spill of oil rolling downriver had paused.

Drone

February 22, 2017

It is said there was a vision the Ghost Dancers saw that made them dance until they fell. It was a little herd of white ponies that seemed like four-winged birds. They hovered in the air over skirmishes. It was the Ghost Dance, after all, when the Seventh Cavalry opened fire. Drones they were, not ponies, first seen by dying Lakota—maybe for a sacred digital library of historical events that have been ignored or forgotten.

The drones over Oceti Sakowin took note of percussion grenades and long-range acoustic devices. The confrontation of security guards, National Guard, police—reminiscent of massacres—Sand Creek. The Washita. Wounded Knee. They said it snowed that day, with thunder and lightning, during evacuation of the resistance camp.

"They shot our drone," I heard two men say. A nonviolent drone with a bullet hole in its underside. It's the same as shooting ponies.

The governor of North Dakota issued the emergency evacuation for the flood plain, saying he worried that protestors might be in danger when the snow melts. Trucks arrived to carry off trash.

They looked for bodies, an officer said, like soldiers after Wounded Knee.

When drilling to carry pipe under the river began, it is said it sounded like the bullets fired in 1890.

PART VIII

NOTHING BUT SKY AND GROUND

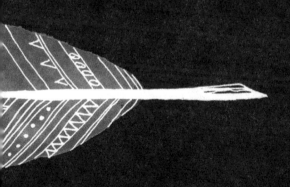

A VIEW FROM THE WINDSHIELD OF MY CAR

A Retrospect

October 5, 2011, on my way from Kansas City to South Dakota on I-29.

Traveling after dark in South Dakota, I saw the harvesters with their bright lights stirring dust in the fields. All day, I had driven on the flat land, longing for description of something other than the plain land. I had driven so long, I came to the same scraped and plain place in myself. The air was dusty with harvesters in fields. I could look straight at the sun with the ring around its center, as if a huge planet sat on the horizon and the heavens were rearranged.

A thin string of clouds seemed to gird the sun, making it look like Mars with a ring around its middle.

In the dark, I stopped at the White Lake rest stop west of Mitchell, and crawled over the seat to lie down in the back of my car. I sleep.

In The Secret History of the Mongol Queens, Jack Weatherford writes about women who traveled. "All carts had the same black covering. . . . Common women drove a lumbering ox or a wooly yak before their heavy laden carts . . . but in her older years, Hoe-lun [the mother of Genghis Kahn] . . . was known to travel long distances very quickly and even to travel at night."

In my dreams, I kept traveling with the earth through the sky. It seemed everything was moving. Even in sleep, I was aware of cars and trucks that entered the rest area, and started out again on the road.

Before the sun came up, I woke. It was a raw, plain dawn. I went into the rest stop and washed my face.

I returned to the car and sat a moment until I was awake.

I've been over these roads before I passed the harvested fields of milo. Corn. Sunflowers. The land disrupted by the farmer's plow.

I thought of my ninety-nine-year-old aunt in Kansas City. In her head, it would be snowing, and the folks were coming from the farm. She should start home any minute. Every time I visit her, she has no idea who I am, or who she is. Neither does she know where she is, or when it is. As she talks, weaving in and out of the past, I recognize her structure and chaos battered by interior wind.

Traveling those distances by myself, I came to see I have been alone after all. Despite the efforts to be with others. Though I have family and activities with others, I am a loner, as maybe everyone discovers. Maybe not. I only can speak what I know. After the dissolution of a marriage in which I put my trust. Or at least, my hope for trust. After I got in line with what I thought I should do. Returned to church. Believed, as maybe I always had.

Along I-90, there was the crossing of the Missouri River, then the wrinkled erosion of the Badlands. The Black Hills. And of course, Wall Drug, for which there had been signs for four hundred miles across South Dakota.

I thought of the lonely road through South Dakota. The fields. The distant farms. Yet there was life buried there. A network I could not see and was not a part of, except my mother's people were farmers in eastern Kansas, and I still felt the string of connectives to them, as did my aged aunt. I think, in these lonely times, I yearned for something significant in the distance beyond which I could see.

From several peaks, I saw the mountains turn blue in the distance, as if becoming a part of the sky. As if putting on the sky as a coat.

I remember the evening sun in South Dakota with a warrior stripe around its middle.

In travel, there were patterns that followed one another. Patterns that followed others before it.

In travel, I picked up distance. Maybe it was not just the land, but the travel over it. I feel the past when I drive. I feel the connections. The land also spoke of its separation from what it was.

I had come to the nomadic life of my later years— and the somber places within myself that travel revealed, as if various points of interest. I found I was nothing connected to nothing but a will to move across the land in the aftermath of flood. The cleanup of standing water—my job and family of my earlier life, bulldozed like the highway along the Missouri River.

I drove I-15 south through Utah and California into San Diego.

Along the drive I saw the mountains turn blue in the distance as if becoming a part of the sky. As if putting on the sky as a coat.

At the University of California / San Diego, I attended a writing conference. In one of the sessions, a young woman presented her paper. She was aban-doned as an infant in a cardboard box. On the table before her was a small cardboard box with a lid. She opened it and picked strips of paper at random, from which she read various aspects of her life. She had defused the difficult experience of her abandonment by fragmenting it.

In my aunt's case, it was what age had done.

When the young woman at the conference read the strips of paper from her cardboard box again, she would pick them in a different order, like memory. It would be as if they were traveling, presenting their different views before a windshield moving across the land.

Travel is a road full of jumping waves connected to the eye of the solar system. Just look at the sun during a total eclipse. The black earth was the pupil, the cornea, or corona. Nothing more than a lumbering ox or wooly yak pulling a cart on a road through the dark.

THE LANGUAGE
OF WEATHER

Weather is an act of revision. Its connotation is changeableness.

Weather must have been anecdote to the boredom and isolation of the farm in Kansas. It was something happening. An active, ongoing state of conflicted activity.

I'm drawn to words with opposite meanings, among them the word weather.

Weather is what is in the air—the atmosphere, with its furniture of heat and cold, clouds and wind.

Weather holds its opposites: −2°F in January; 102° in July. Blizzard, downpour, and/or drought.

Besides what's going on in the air, to weather means to wear away. Weather weathered the boards on my grandfather's barn and outbuildings.

The word, *weather*, means to survive. My grandfather weathered the storms on a farm in Bourbon County, Kansas. I visited as a child in the 1940s. Like the weather, the farm stayed with me through the years.

Weather, from the Indo-European word for wind, or to blow, wee. There were nights we listened to the wind roar as we tried to sleep.

The etymology includes vedra/vedro—Danish/old Slavic words meaning good weather.

There's also the German word, wetter.

All of the sounds and their breezy meanings went into the shaping of the word, weather.

It's a word with a large, metal hinge—gray as the dust blowing from the road and field in drought. Gray as a sky full of rain.

Identical in sound is *whether*—with its own bifurcated meaning, which of two. Something that can go one way. Or another. One that has two ways within it. Or actually more than two ways to go, like the dust lifting from a field has options from the wind for which direction or directions it will blow.

Weather was the fearful other on the farm without electricity. It brought incoming storms that must have been their Saturday-night movies, although storms could happen any weeknight, or become an afternoon matinee, for that matter, when storm clouds filled the sky above the open farm. My aunts were afraid of the storms.

Discomfort was yet another meaning of weather.

There was no hand fan big enough to cool the hot upstairs room with its swaying floor.

There wasn't even a quilt, hand-stitched from old material scraps, heavy enough to truly warm us.

Other than weather and their four children, these were my grandfather's possessions:

> Animals—pigs, chickens, cows, horse.
> Land—a pasture, corn field, and pond.
> Farmhouse, barn, outbuildings, and cellar.

Air—where the weather lived with its extremes.

All of it—except the weather—isolated on a long dirt road that went to Highway 69 to the west, or Crossroad 239 over the state line into Hume, Missouri, to the east.

My house in Kansas is made of weatherboards. Clapboards. Overlapping boards.

Inside my house are a few small implements from the farm, which are my inheritance—an ice pick, a wooden potato masher, a small wheel that served as a pulley in the barn.

There is weather stripping in the doors and windows—a thin, metal strip covering the joint between sash and jamb, casing and sill, to keep out drafts. When the wind blows in a certain way, it vibrates the weather stripping in a wheeze of metal.

Weather itself is a large, misshapen object passing through a name that sounds as narrow as feather.

I stand at an opened window watching the lighting—waiting for its companion, the thunder. I'm attracted to storms—feeling the cool wind after a hot afternoon. I stand there until rain comes in as if it was invited.

In winter, I stand at the window, watching snow.

Weather contains the elements of my imagination, the language of my atmosphere—my love of land, isolation, the constancy of travel, and change.

I love the weather because it is the language of the sun. It speaks to the Earth unevenly because the

Earth is round. The sun shines more directly on the face of the globe, leaving the north and south poles with less heat.

When temperatures are not the same, they begin to argue. The unevenness causes air currents that redistribute heat. Wind pushes and shoves, much like four children in a farmhouse in winter. This is mine. No, it is mine. Give it to me. Tilting and spinning the farmhouse over and over. A hot core somewhere erupting. A cold front from the north.

Weather is a little army saying, charge.

From Wikipedia:

Generally speaking, there are two main modes of heat redistribution.

Vertical heat transport: Solar heating of the Earth's surface makes the atmosphere convectively unstable, causing vertical air currents to develop.

Horizontal heat transport: Because the Earth is a sphere [it receives uneven light, which] causes horizontal temperature differences to develop, which in turn causes air pressure differences, leading to wind that transports heat from the tropics to the high latitudes.

Together, this uneven heating in both the horizontal and vertical directions in the atmosphere cause what we know as weather.

EARLY WINTER

Let us try to read the larger lettering.
—*Cliffs Notes*, Book II Section II, Plato's *Republic*

On I-35 in Kansas, south and a little west of where my grandfather's farm had been, the Flint Hills rise above the land. It is mostly a barren place. The sky pales. The ground is russet. Maybe darkened by range burning. But with a glint of something other than brown. A muted brightness. A nothingness that is enveloping. For a moment, I have a flash of the old farm. Or one of the photographs of it. Nothing but sky and ground. A fence. My grandfather and I standing by a calf. Nothing else and nothing else.

You see cattle grazing in the distance in the Flint Hills. The summer is spent. On its last leg. No migrating flocks flying over a steady roll of land of no particular notice in its plainness, its lostness from what is known. To what could it be compared? The few trees on the Flint Hills like capital letters standing in a sentence? What similitude when the exact truth of it is beyond words? Only the disquiet of the void that brings it to notice. A nothing that intervenes. The sky empty even of clouds. Of plane.

I pass the Flint Hills often, in travels to a daughter and her family in Kansas, a son and his family in Texas.

Much as the weather, travel is oppositional. My constant driving, 482 miles for seven and a half hours from Kansas to Texas, Texas to Kansas. On one trip, I broke into the momentum of travel on I-35. I stopped in the Flint Hills at a turnout to look at the evening sky. It was magenta and black. I felt what it was to stand still in the momentum of driving that has swept my life, and my writing, leaving them like the farmhouse, in the constant tangle of currents at odds.

But if I write it, as I do now, as I've done little by little over the years, I could re-defy the edges, the tangle of weather. I could enter the plain Flint Hills the way Plato entered the grove outside Athens, where he lectured. Maybe it was Plato I saw among the branches of clouds low in the sky as it darkened that evening I stopped in the Flint Hills.

In my years of travel, there has been little stopping. The road is a Mobius strip, back and forth across the country. Now at the turnout, I felt a stasis that revealed what is to come. The necessary times between travel that will grow longer.

The old farm of my grandparents still returns as a rerun. The sky, now part of the farm. The moon and stars are in their pasture. The car in the shed for the night with the old farm wagon. The horse, long gone, trots with the solar winds as a harness. The largeness of sky and land. The smallness.

Even in darkness on the road again, the land is barren—nothing seems to hold the traffic that passes in the stream of night. The whole universe—an act of opposition and charged currents. An act of disobedience.

ACKNOWLEDGMENTS

Ambition, an anthology of essays by members of the Chrysostom Society, Luci Shaw, and Jeanne Murray Walker, editors Wipf and Stock, 2015, for "The Move," under the title "Dreams Are Dangerous. They Uncover Your Bones."

Apogee Journal, "#NoDAPL Still Here: Native and Anticolonial Craft Against Dispossession," December 2016 issue, for "Room on My Dance Card."

"Room on My Dance Card" was read October 16, 2016, at a benefit at the Institute of American Indian Arts in Santa Fe, New Mexico, that raised nearly $1,000 for Sacred Stone Camp.

Bat City, University of Texas at Austin, for "Why the Rocks Have Ears"; acknowledgment to Nick Almeida Miller for development of the piece.

College of Arts and Sciences, Azusa Pacific University, Opening Convocation for "The Marching in the Tops of the Mulberry Trees," September 2013.

Encore for "Wolf Lays Down" from "The Marching in the Tops of the Mulberry Trees."

Conference on Christianity and Literature, Western Region, Azusa Pacific University, May 17, 2013, for the Keynote Speech, "Intrusions."

East Wind, Azusa Pacific University, for "Kansas."

ACKNOWLEDGMENTS

The piece also was published in *Transmotion*, http://journals.kent.ac.uk/index.php/transmotion, a biannual, fully and permanently open-access journal inspired by the work of the Anishinaabe writer, Gerald Vizenor, editors James Mackay, David J. Carlson, David Stirrup, and Laura Adams Weaver.

Fourth Genre for "The Writing of Travel—The Travel of Writing," "The Language of Weather," "The Trip to Kansas," and "The Trip Back to California."

Ginosko for "This Village Called a River."

Kenyon Review, literary activism issue, John Kinsella and Rita Dove, editors, December 2019, for the section, "#NoDAPL."

MLA Panel, Post Indian Poses, 2016, Austin, Texas, for "Totem."

Transmotion http://journals.kent.ac.uk/index.php/transmotion, for "Totem."

National Civil War Project Theatrical Event: Our War [twenty-five playwrights invited to write a ten-minute monologue], Arena Stage, Washington, DC, October 21–November 9, 2014, for the theater piece, "Woods Lewis, a Civil War Soldier, and a Grapefruit," published also on the Arena Stage website.

Native American Literature Symposium, March 12–14, 2015, Albuquerque, New Mexico, for *Four Quarters*, and a showing of the independent film.

Nowhere for "A View from the Windshield of My Car."

ACKNOWLEDGMENTS

Red Ink, international journal of indigenous literature, arts & humanities, Arizona State University, for "Even the Stones Speak" under the title, "Brown Paper Bag."

The Windhover issue 23.2 for "Notes to the Joint Staff of Chiefs."

Twenty-First Century Perspectives on Indigenous Studies: Native North America in (Trans)motion, edited by Birgit Daewes, Karsten Fitz, and Sabine Meyers, Routledge, New York, 2015, for "Native Dramatic Theory in a Bird House."

A part of the chapter was read at the Associated Writing Programs Conference, Minneapolis, April 10, 2015, on a panel, Documenting Disasters across Genres, Projects that Investigate Industrial Disasters: Research and Writing Method.

The AWP paper also was published in *Red Ink*, Issue 18.1, Spring 2016.

Hemispheric Institute Digital Video Library, hidvl. nyu.edu/video0003335394.html, for a discussion of the Native concept of language used in English in drama.

Works cited in *The Bird House*:
Black Elk Speaks: Being the Life Story of a Holy Man of the Oglala Sioux, as told through John G. Neihardt, University of Nebraska Press, Lincoln, Nebraska, 1932, 1961, 1979, 1988, with a Premier Edition, SUNY Press, Albany, New York, 2008.

ACKNOWLEDGMENTS

American Gypsy, Six Native American Plays, Diane Glancy, American Indian Literature and Critical Studies Series #45, University of Oklahoma Press, Norman, Oklahoma, 2002.

Gratefulness also to Lil Copan and Broadleaf Books.